MW00988095

THE 101 BEST

Freshwater Nano Species

THE ADVENTUROUS AQUARIST™ GUIDE SERIES

Produced and distributed by:

TFH Publications, Inc.
One TFH Plaza
Third and Union Avenues
Neptune City, NJ 07753
www.tfh.com

Printed and bound in China
15 16 17 18   5 7 9 8 6 4 2

ISBN-13:   978-0-9820262-5-0
ISBN-10:   0-9820262-5-0
UPC-A: 6-81290-02625-5

Edited by James M. Lawrence
Designed by Linda Provost
Production: Anne Linton Elston
Contributing Editor: Mary E. Sweeney
Copyediting: Louise Watson, Alex Bunten
Business Manager: Judith R. Billard

A MICROCOSM/TFH Professional Series Book

TFH Publications, Inc.
Neptune City, NJ 07753
www.tfh.com
MICROCOSM, Ltd
Shelburne, VT 05482
www.reef2rainforest.com

THE 101 BEST

Freshwater Nano Species

HOW TO CHOOSE & KEEP HARDY,

BRILLIANT, FASCINATING SPECIES

THAT WILL THRIVE IN YOUR

SMALL AQUARIUM

Text and photography by
MARK DENARO
& RACHEL O'LEARY

With additional images by
Hans-Georg Evers, Dr. Paul V. Loiselle, Gary Lange,
Aaron Norman, MP & C Piednoir, and Sumer Tiwari

MICROCOSM

tfh

PROFESSIONAL
SERIES™

THE ADVENTUROUS AQUARIST™ GUIDE SERIES

A MICROCOSM/TFH PROFESSIONAL SERIES EDITION

WWW.REEF2RAINFOREST.COM/MICROCOSM-BOOKS

Cover Photograph
by Hans-Georg Evers

Front: Forktail Blue-Eye Rainbow
(*Pseudomugil furcatus*), page 136

Back: Top — Electric Blue German Ram, page 94, Gary Lange
Middle — Planted Nano Tank, page 21, Sumer Tiwari
Bottom — Green Shrimp, page 173, Rachel O'Leary
Spine: Spotted Blue-Eye Rainbow, page 137, Hans-Georg Evers

ACKNOWLEDGMENTS

I'd like to thank my wife, Donna, and my daughters, Jeanne, Melanie, and Lucy, who have long suffered from my affliction, I mean interest, in aquariums, and who've come to understand that vacations mean going to a fish convention and then spending a few extra days or going somewhere that has a public aquarium or a place to collect fish. They not only tolerate my interest in fish but encourage it as well.

I'd also like to acknowledge the role of my parents, Joseph and Theora Denaro, who never understood my obsession with fish but finally stopped asking, "When are you going to get a real job?"

This book would not have been possible without the people who have mentored me in the hobby. They are far too many to mention but a few stand out. Three of the first people I met when I found the wonderful world of the organized hobby and joined the Indianapolis Aquarium Society in 1984 profoundly impacted my transition from a kid who had fish tanks into a professional aquarist. I want to thank Al Anderson, Charley Grimes, and Vern Parish for spending innumerable hours answering questions and showing me what they were doing that made their fishrooms so successful—and making sure I understood why the things they were doing worked.

—Mark Denaro

First and foremost I would like to thank my husband, Chris, who worked tirelessly to build my fishroom and whose patience, love, and support during all my travels is unparalleled, especially for someone who does not "do" fish. I would like to thank my daughters, Abby and Clelia, for their constant companionship on the aquarium club circuit. Many thanks to all my friends and customers, especially my fellow board members of the Capital Cichlid Association, my current aquarium club. Many people have helped me along the way, including peers and mentors like my co-author, Mark Denaro; Ricky Chawla and Bill Brissette, who provided ceaseless editing and web help; supportive good friends like Whitney Sumerix, Anthony Horos, Chris Biggs, and Ray Quennelle; and my number one fans, Gavin Dalton and Sheila Garl. Special thanks to Hans-Georg Evers, who always finds the time to answer my questions and give a friendly word. Lastly, I would like to acknowledge my appreciation for my late mother, Pam Scott, who gave me unflagging encouragement.

—Rachel O'Leary

CONTENTS

Spotted Blue-Eye Rainbow (Pseudomugil gertrudae), *page 137*

CONTENTS

Quick Species Finders......... Inside Front & Back Covers

Meant as a field guide to nano-aquarium species, this guide uses color photographs taken in home aquariums for quick visual identification. Species appearing here have been selected as outstanding for their hardiness and durability in aquarium conditions, and for their attractiveness and interesting behaviors.

Fishes, plants, and freshwater invertebrates are arranged alphabetically by genus name within their family groupings.

In addition to a species overview and notes about aquarium behaviors and compatibility, each account contains concise facts and advice, organized as follows:

COMMON NAME

In this guide, one or more common names are listed for each species. The first name provided is the name most frequently used in the authoritative checklists and field guides written by ichthyologists, botanists, and zoologists. Alternate common names used in the aquarium trade are included wherever appropriate.

SCIENTIFIC NAME

This is the most current name applied to the fish by the scientific community. The name is in the form of a binomial. The first name indicates the genus to which the organism belongs, while the second is the species name. When common names are confusing, the scientific name is a benchmark that all can understand. For example, *Akysis vespa* is the scientific name for the Orangebanded Hillstream Catfish, and it goes by all of these common names: Wasp Catfish, Orangebanded Stone Catfish, Micro Bumblebee Catfish, and others. The scientific name often provides clarity with the genus being a clue to the traits and keeping requirements of other closely related species grouped within that genus.

MAXIMUM LENGTH

This indicates the greatest standard length that an individual of that particular species can attain—or the longest ever reported—measuring from the end of the snout to the base of the tail. In most cases, the length of an aquarium specimen will fall short of this measure; nonetheless, the aquarist should always plan for the prospect of his or her fish reaching a maximum length close to that presented.

NATIVE RANGE
This entry notes the broad geographical area where each species occurs. The distribution of a fish is of great value to aquarists wishing to set up a tank that represents a natural community or biotope from a certain geographical region.

MINIMUM AQUARIUM SIZE
This is the minimum suitable aquarium volume for an adult individual of the species. Of course, juveniles and adolescents can be housed in smaller tanks. Activity levels and behavior patterns of a particular species have been accounted for whenever possible. The suggested sizes given throughout this book must be regarded as the minimum, and providing more space and water volume will allow any fish to acclimate better and display less aggression toward its tankmates, as well as providing more stable water chemistry and temperature.

FEEDING
The feeding preferences and requirements of fishes and invertebrates vary dramatically. Advice in this section includes the type of foods generally preferred by the species. Feeding a variety of foods is recommended for most aquarium species. Unless otherwise noted, most fishes should be fed twice daily with portions that are completely consumed within three minutes.

Meaty foods for carnivorous fishes and micropredators include dried and frozen aquarium foods, including brine (*Artemia*) shrimp, mysid (*Mysis*) shrimp, *Cyclops*, *Daphnia*, rotifers, worms of various types, and others. High quality prepared rations may contain ingredients for both carnivores and herbivores.

Live foods include adult or newly hatched brine shrimp (*Artemia*), *Daphnia*, *Cyclops*, Grindal worms, white worms, black worms, bloodworms, mosquito larvae, and many other items from pet shops. *Daphnia* and *Cyclops* are easily cultured as well as readily available; they're some of the very best foods.

Herbivore foods include dried and frozen preparations that contain unicellular algae (especially *Spirulina*) and various types of red, green, and brown marine algae. Many aquarists feed table vegetables, such as spinach, zucchini, broccoli, or even carrots. These are usually microwaved, blanched, or frozen and thawed before feeding. Because of the high possibility of contamination with pesticides, supermarket produce should be regarded with suspicion. Homegrown or organic vegetables are much more trustworthy.

Color enhancers are now recommended for many, if not all, aquarium fishes. An increasing number of rations contain added vitamins and pigments, such as carotenoids, to help maintain fishes' naturally bright colors.

Live plants are an important source of food for some species. Many protozoans, crustaceans, worms, and micro- and macroalgae reproduce on plant leaves, and these will supplement the diets of many nano-fishes and invertebrates.

HABITAT

Many fishes will do best in aquariums aquascaped to replicate the biotopes they inhabit in the wild. Some need heavy plantings to thrive, many others only acclimate well when provided with a profusion of caves and hiding places to give them a sense of security. Driftwood and rock can improve the well-being of many species and have a purpose beyond simple aesthetics. Having the proper habitat is a major stress-reliever for most aquarium animals.

A portal into the world of small aquariums and nano-aquatic species

What is a nano-aquarium? Ten aquarium-keepers may give you ten different answers, so we need to set some parameters. For the purpose of this volume, we are defining freshwater nano-aquariums as tanks with a capacity of 20 gallons or less. While this size is smaller than the size typically used in the marine side of the hobby, it is still large enough that it includes the aquariums most commonly purchased by new hobbyists, i.e., 10-gallon and 20-gallon (38–76-L) tanks. It is important to note that while this volume includes some classic beginner species, it is not intended as a primer on freshwater fishes. If that is the book you are looking for, see *The 101 Best Tropical Fishes*, by Kathleen Wood, or *The PocketExpert Guide to Tropical Fishes,* by Mary E. Sweeney, Mary Bailey, and Aaron Norman.

Our intention is to give hobbyists with some experience ideas that they can put into practice in creating vibrant, dynamic nano-aquariums. It is up to you to know your limitations and not attempt to keep species that have specific, difficult-to-meet requirements that are suitable only for experienced hobbyists until you are confident in your ability to meet their needs and properly care for them.

The typical first aquarium is decorated with a few artificial plants and an ornament or two. These are usually placed haphazardly and the overall effect is rarely aesthetically pleasing. Still, many hobbyists have success with these setups and then they tend to move on to more and larger aquariums, and over time their ability to decorate their tanks improves. It's only later that they go back to smaller tanks, this time with a different perspective and a different objective: creating an attractive, viable aquascape that will be populated with a few specific species of fish and aquascaped with live plants. Other hobbyists start with small tanks and continue to keep small tanks even when they add more. This could be due to space considerations, budget, or a host of other reasons. For these hobbyists, too, the perspective tends to change and they will want to improve the look of their tanks and ensure that the species

A nano-tank can be home to an amazing array of plants and aquatic animals.

they're keeping will do well. Some potential aquarists are attracted to the hobby specifically because they've seen a very striking nano-tank somewhere along the line and they want to create something like it in their home or office. It is for these folks that we've included some of the typical beginner fishes. Of course, even some very experienced hobbyists may be inspired by reading a profile on a fish they kept years ago or one they skipped when they started out.

In addition to fishes, this volume includes bonus profiles of some of the best invertebrates and plants for the freshwater nano-aquarium. In recent years, we've seen an incredible influx of invertebrates into the hobby. The diversity of shrimp and snails is hard to imagine for those of us who started out in the days when the available invertebrates were ghost shrimp, mystery snails, ramshorn snails, and occasionally crayfish. Immersing oneself in the fascinating world of shrimp requires some advance research and an understanding of how their requirements differ from those of fishes.

This volume will prepare you to keep these wonderful animals successfully. There are probably 600 varieties of plants available to aquarium-keepers on a regular basis, so figuring out which ones to choose can be a daunting task. The species included in this book are all very good choices for nano-sized tanks, and the information included should give you a starting point for planning your aquascape.

Some hobbyists will want to breed the fishes and invertebrates that they are keeping, and this presents additional challenges. In most cases, a species tank is required for successful spawning and additional aquariums may be needed to rear the resulting fry. Setting up an aquarium using the principles set forth in this volume may result in the spawning of many species, but specific information on successfully reproducing all the species included is beyond the scope of this book.

Planning and equipping
a freshwater nano-aquarium

Nano-aquariums come in a variety of shapes and sizes, so it is important to carefully plan your aquarium prior to purchasing the tank. Tanks of the same capacity may have very different shapes, so you should consider a number of factors prior to purchase.

First, where will the aquarium be located? Is the location subject to fluctuations in temperature? We're dealing with small volumes of water, so changing room temperature can have a significant impact. Water acts as a heat sink or reservoir and will maintain its temperature fairly well, but that is increasingly true with increasing volume and not so true in nano-tanks. This is especially important to consider when the aquarium is being placed in a commercial building. Is the heat or air conditioning turned off on weekends or is it set to a more economical level? Mysterious fish deaths in commercial buildings can frequently be attributed to weekend temperature fluctuations. These can also stress the animals and weaken their resistance to disease. Will the location receive natural sunlight?

Most aquarium retailers now offer a wide selection of nano-tanks, filters, lighting, and accessories, as well as complete nano-systems in a single box.

While not a bad idea in every situation, natural sunlight causes more problems than it solves with nano-tanks. Temperature fluctuation can be an issue, as the sunlight will heat the aquarium. Sunlight can also cause undesirable algae growth, particularly if there are excess nutrients available in the system.

Second, how will the aquarium be supported? Will it be placed on a stand designed specifically to hold it or will it sit on another piece of furniture? If it will be placed on a dresser or table or shelf, will that piece of furniture support the weight? While a gallon of water weighs 8.3 pounds, one must also consider the weight of the aquarium, gravel, décor, and equipment. A good rule of thumb is to estimate the system weight at 10 pounds per gallon. This becomes very significant as we approach the larger end of our range, where a fully set up 20-gallon aquarium weighs somewhere around 200 pounds. In addition to being sure that the stand/furniture will support the weight, don't forget to measure to make sure the aquarium will fit. There's nothing worse than bringing home a 24"-long tank to find that its intended location is only 22" long.

Third, what species will be maintained? The species that one desires to maintain affect the size and shape of the aquarium, and this is true of plants as well as animals. If the desire is for a back wall of relatively tall stem plants, a taller tank is more desirable. For active, schooling fishes or territorial fishes that need to set up their boundaries on the bottom, longer, shallower tanks are preferred. Shallower, longer tanks also have a higher surface-area-to-volume ratio, so the dissolved oxygen level is higher with that shape. This can be important with some of the cool-temperature and faster water-flow species, like the hillstream loaches and some of the danionins. It is always best to plan the community before purchasing the aquarium.

Fourth, how will the aquarium be filtered? The answer to this question is, to at least some extent, determined by the answer to the third question. In most aquariums, filtration should be thought of as a triangle with three equally important sides. Mechanical filtration traps particles and collects them in media such as filter floss, a foam block, or a 100-micron bag. The particulates are then easily removed from the system by changing or cleaning the mechanical filter material. Biological filtration utilizes bacteria to break down

If you intend to grow a profusion of plants, be sure to acquire good LED or compact fluorescent lighting, ideally mounted above the tank, not in the hood.

the wastes of our inhabitants, as well as excess food and dead leaves, etc., into a series of compounds. The potentially highly toxic ammonia is broken down by *Nitrosomonas* and similar bacteria into rather toxic nitrite, which is then oxidized by *Nitrobacter* and similar bacteria into nitrate, which is relatively less toxic. The monkey wrench in the biological filtration side of the triangle is water chemistry. In low pH water, bacterial activity is significantly impacted, and in aquariums set up to mimic blackwater habitats, little to no biological filtration is possible. The bright side is that the form that ammonia takes is determined by pH and the form taken in low-pH water is exponentially less toxic to fishes and invertebrates. In that situation, chemical filtration becomes more important than it is in most other aquariums.

Chemical filtration removes dissolved organics and other undesirable chemical compounds by adsorbing them. Some common products that are used for chemical filtration include activated carbon and ion exchange resins, which can be a single resin intended to remove one specific thing, or mixed-bed resins that are more cosmopolitan in their removal abilities, or combinations of chemicals. There are also a variety of products intended to remove things like nitrate or silicate, which can be very useful in limiting or eliminating algae growth. More advanced products use polymers to remove all these things plus ammonia—obviously a great thing when biological filtration is ineffective, but they can also help tank inhabitants survive with less stress at higher pH while the biological filtration is becoming established or has been compromised. Every aquarium should have some form of mechanical filtration and chemical filtration and, if it will work, biological filtration.

Fifth, how will the aquarium be lit? There are numerous options, and the preferred methods have changed in the time since the popularity of nano-tanks began to grow. An important consideration when choosing lighting is the amount of heat produced. Heat produced by the lighting system can cause temperature fluctuations in an inverse relationship to tank size. If this is a problem in your tank, the simplest solution is to raise the light fixture so that it is further away from the tank—but this decreases the amount of light penetrating the water. In most cases, the best option is probably LED lighting. Other options include compact fluorescent lights, T5

Colorado aquarist Sumer Tiwari calls this a "bird's eye view" of his 18-gallon planted nano-aquarium, with lush plant growth under bright LED lighting.

fluorescent bulbs in regular and high output options, 'standard' fluorescents, and incandescents.

LED technology offers the advantages of relatively cool operation, which will not transfer enough heat to the water to cause fluctuations in water temperature; low power consumption; and incredibly long bulb life. A side benefit is that the light produced by these systems will shimmer or refract due to surface movement, which gives the aquascape a much more natural look and is considered aesthetically appealing by most hobbyists. These systems may be more expensive to purchase than some of the other options, but their operating costs will generally make them the best choice for the long term.

Compact fluorescent setups can be more intense than LEDs but they produce more heat and cost more to operate, and the bulbs don't last nearly as long; the same is true for T5 bulbs. Standard fluorescents are sufficient for low to medium light setups, but if the desire is for demanding plants with high light requirements they are insufficient. Incandescent lighting is inexpensive to install, but the high heat produced, high power consumption, and frequent need to replace the bulbs make it a poor choice in most cases. It will also shimmer, though, so it can be very attractive. There are some spectacular planted tanks out there lit solely by incandescent light, so despite the fact that this technology is not in vogue with hobbyists, it can work well. *Cryptocoryne* species in particular seem to do very well under this lighting.

With the increasing popularity of nano-aquariums, many manufacturers now offer boxed kits with the tank, filtration, and lighting included and designed to work together. Some manufacturers go so far as to market nano-fish tanks and nano-shrimp tanks separately and add to their repertoire by offering systems designed specifically to maximize plant growth. That may even include plant-specific substrate and a basic CO_2 system.

In many instances, purchasing these kits is a very simple option that will help the hobbyist on his or her way to success. The downside is that some of them are better suited to marine setups than freshwater setups. If the filtration is built into a hidden compartment in the back of the aquarium and includes some type of trickle filter, one of its functions is to drive out CO_2 to maximize dissolved oxygen levels. This is a great thing in marine aquariums and may be a good thing for freshwater fishes, but it is decidedly bad for plants.

Fortunately, more and more kits are including internal or hang-on filters, which are easy to maintain and service. The hobbyist who prefers to think outside the kit box can purchase a standard aquarium in any desired (and available) shape and size. Those who are handy can build their tanks out of acrylic or glass, making the dimensions limited only by the available space. Using acrylic opens additional options in terms of colors, so the back, bottom, and sides can be black or any other desired color. Building the tank means that the aquarist has to make more decisions and not just accept the decisions made by the manufacturer whose kit he/she purchases. This provides greater flexibility in matching the filtration and lighting to the needs of the inhabitants.

Open aquarium kits are another option, and these can be stunning when well planned and executed. These systems typically have a front panel that is shorter than the side and back panels. The idea is to have an aquarium with driftwood or rocks that stick up out of the water, with epiphytic plants attached to the wood or rocks. Plants in the water section can also be allowed to grow out of the tank to add to the interest above the surface.

A very pleasing nano-aquascape with low-growing plants in the foreground and taller species at the back wall makes use of a plant-fertilizing substrate

Creating an underwater world in nano scale

Now that the equipment has been assembled, it's time to set up the aquarium. Start by making sure that the stand or other support structure is level. Next, rinse or wipe the tank with water. Do not use any soap or chemicals to clean the tank. At this point some very significant decisions must be made.

How do you want the aquarium to look? The decision you make right now with regard to aquascaping is the most important decision you'll make in reference to this aquarium. This decision will affect how much time and effort is involved in maintenance and will determine the type and amount of lighting and filtration required. While most of the information in this volume is geared toward creating a natural system with live plants, you may want to choose artificial plants or other items to decorate your tank, and that is perfectly acceptable. If you do want a natural-looking aquascape, there are several options from which to choose. A biotope tank will recreate a natural ecosystem using plants and animals that would be found together in nature. If a biotope is not for you, there are two primary schools of thought about creating planted aquascapes. Leiden or Dutch style aquariums are densely planted and reminiscent of formal gardens. Typically included in these setups is the use of an avenue or "*Leiden Strasse*" created by diagonally planting a group of a single species in which the height of the plants increases toward the back of the tank. This is a very effective method for drawing the viewer into the tank. The other option is the nature aquarium method popularized by Takashi Amano in which a terrestrial biotope is replicated in the aquarium.

There is no wrong choice here. Choose the approach that appeals most to your sense of aesthetics. If you are creating a biotope aquarium, search the Internet for pictures of the area you want to recreate or, better yet, visit it yourself to see what is truly there and how it is arranged. If you can't travel to the tropics, get out to your local streams or lakes. Looking at natural biotopes will inspire your

The end result of the step-by-step process shown on the following pages, this 8-gallon (30-L) "nano-cube" comes as a complete kit with all components.

Intended to support thriving plants, this nano-creation starts with a bottom layer of iron-rich laterite substrate. See previous pages for the final result of this aquarium kit setup.

Next, a layer of dark substrate is added and leveled. This is one of a number of new plant-specific subtrates that incorporate a slow-release fertilizer.

design ideas and give you a better appreciation of how a natural biotope truly looks. This can be useful for any of your aquascaping choices. If you're using the nature aquarium approach, take (or find) a picture of the location you'd like to replicate. Having the picture to work from makes recreating it much simpler. While many of the elements discussed below relate specifically to the Leiden style aquascape, they should also be considered when creating a biotope or nature aquarium. It is most important to be true to the area you are recreating in these systems, but this can be done using the following design considerations.

There are two very important rules to consider before planning any aquascape. First, never place a focal point in the center of the aquarium. This causes the viewer to try to see symmetry in the overall aquascape and is not aesthetically pleasing. Second is a rule we borrow from floral designers: hide your mechanics. This should be your mantra. Nothing detracts more from an aquascape than seeing the filtration or CO_2 unit or airline or any other artificial addition.

There should be three focal points in the aquascape, with two on one side and one on the other. If the aquarium will be viewed from the left, two of these focal points should be on the right side of the tank, and vice versa. Placing the focal points there will help to draw the viewer's eye into the aquarium. If the aquarium will

Hardscaping with driftwood and stone can be done before water is added to allow the aquarist to try different aquascaping approaches before settling on a final look for the tank.

Water is now poured in slowly, using a plate or shallow bowl to prevent disturbing the substrate so you don't end up with cloudy water that can take a day to clear.

be viewed from directly in front, the placement of the focal points is completely at your discretion. One focal point should be in the foreground, one in the middle ground, and one in the background in order to draw the viewer all the way into the aquarium. Focal points should be placed at the angles of a golden triangle. This ratio is commonly used in design and has been known since the time of Pythagoras. While the math may seem daunting, the ratio is built into the human brain, and once you're aware of it and have used it to design a few aquascapes it will be so natural that you won't have to think about it. A golden triangle is an isosceles triangle ABC in which in which sides AB and AC are the same length, with side BC being a different length. I'm sure that everyone can picture that, but here's the tricky part. If you bisect the angle at point C and draw a line from there that connects to the AB side of the original triangle, the new, smaller triangle that you have created will be similar to the original triangle. Another way to envision this is to take a pentagon and draw lines connecting all the corner points. Doing this will create 10 triangles. All the acute triangles (all angles less than 90 degrees) will be golden triangles

If you are using a very small tank and only have room for two focal points, you can determine the ideal placement for those by using the golden ratio, which is also known as the golden section.

Planting is started before filling the aquarium to minimize spillage. Nano-aquarium planting and maintenance tools are available and handy, but not required for success.

Some trial and error comes into play as the aquascape takes shape and plants are rearranged until the aquarist is satisfied.

The golden ratio is a mathematical constant, first described by Euclid and used regularly in art and design. The ratio is 1.6180339887 to 1. If you divide the length and width of your tank by 2.6180339887 you can determine where to place the focal points. For example, in a 10-gallon (38-L) tank (20 x 10 x 12 inches / 51 x 25 x 30 cm), your rear focal point should be located 7.6 inches in from one end of the tank and 3.8 inches in from the rear. The other focal point should be 7.6 inches in from the opposite end and 3.8 inches in from the front of the tank.

After you have determined where to place your focal points, it is time to lay out the rest of the aquascape. At this time, it is best to make a drawing of the aquarium. Include the approximate size and shape of any driftwood or rocks that you will be using. If you're incorporating a plant avenue, remember that this can be one of your focal points. Red plants make excellent focal points, as do showy specimen plants like *Nymphaea* species or a Black Amazon Swordplant, *E. parviflorus*. Rocks and driftwood can also be used as focal points. Now for the fun part: choosing a selection of plants that will accentuate your focal points and each other. It is important to contrast the color and shape of the leaves when you plan the tank. For example, if your background planting is a group of *Vallisneria*, with green, grass-like leaves, the aquarium will look best if the plants

Mechanical equipment, including the filter and CO_2 dosing system, if included, are now installed. Creative use of driftwood or rock can often hide the presence of such gear.

The tank in its final position, with lighting installed and water level topped up. Before adding any livestock, it is best to let the system establish itself.

in front of the Val exhibit horizontally growing leaves of a different color, or at least a different shade of green. A stem or "bunch" plant might be a very good choice, and a species with a different color will be particularly ideal—so maybe *Rotala rotundifolia* should be planted here. In front of the *Rotala*, you may want to refer back to the Val by using a plant with grass-type leaves, so your choices might include one of the smaller-growing chain swordplants. You'll also need to contrast the color and shape of each plant species with those of the ones planted next to, behind, and in front of them.

Are you using driftwood in your aquascape? If so, is it waterlogged or sufficiently dense that it will sink? If not, it should be attached to the tank so that it doesn't suddenly pop up and knock the lights into the aquarium. The traditional method of attaching a piece of slate to the wood and then burying that in the substrate, so that the weight of the gravel holds the wood down, is particularly unwieldy in a nano-system. The best choice is to determine where the wood will make contact with the bottom, sides, and back wall of the tank and screw suction cups into the wood at those points to hold it in place. Two to four suction cups should be sufficient for the size of wood appropriate in a nano-aquarium. Attaching the wood to the back and/or end of the tank in addition to the bottom will dramatically increase its stability. I usually use zinc screws. If the wood

Stone can be used to create natural-looking hardscapes to be enhanced by plantings, as in this 15-gallon "Iwagumi-style" (rock formation) nano tank.

is particularly dense, it can be quite helpful to drill pilot holes first. Suction cups can be purchased in the crafts section of a department store. Before you screw them into the wood, try placing the wood in different locations in the tank and at different angles to determine its best placement. Wet the suction cups and attach the wood to the tank prior to adding the substrate so that it can adhere directly to the tank. Alternatively, the wood can be soaked until it sinks. Small pieces can also be boiled, which will increase the speed with which they become waterlogged.

The substrate you choose will provide the base for the whole aquascape, so a lot of thought should go into this decision. Natural gravel should be the choice if you want the tank to look like a slice of nature. Dark substrates are preferred in almost all cases. Many fishes can adjust their color patterns to at least some degree, and dark substrates encourage brighter colors; the same fishes may appear washed out over a light substrate. Ideally, the substrate should be very fine-grained and can go into the realm of sand. Large-grained substrates simply don't look right in small aquariums.

There are a variety of products on the market that are intended to be used in planted aquariums. These work well, but a better option in many cases is to use a more inert substrate and add iron-rich clay, like a laterite-based product. This allows the hobbyist to control the amount added and tailor it to the anticipated planting level. The big advantage to this approach is that it should cut down on algae growth, particularly when the aquarium is first set up and the plants are not yet well established. The depth of the substrate is dependent upon the plants chosen and the plan of the aquascape. The absolute minimum depth is 1 inch, but 2 is better. The substrate can be flat or gently sloping from deeper at the back to shallower in the front. Dramatic effects can be achieved by significantly varying the depth of the substrate. Rocks or driftwood can be used to hold the gravel in place and create hills or mountains with the substrate. This is particularly effective in taller tanks. If the substrate you choose is on the dusty side, it may be a good idea to wash it first. Place a small amount in a bucket and run water into the bucket while swirling the substrate to get the fine particles into suspension so they can be poured out.

Rocks can be added before or after the substrate, depending on how they will be placed and if they're being used for any purpose other than decoration. If the rocks will be used to hold the substrate, they must be added prior to the substrate. The rocks you choose must be appropriately sized for the aquarium, and also must be safe for the livestock. You can ensure this by purchasing rock from your local aquarium shop. You can also collect your own from local streams; most rocks found there will be safe. If the rock has any shiny or metallic areas it probably isn't safe and should not be used. One way to test it is to put a bit of vinegar or muriatic acid on it. If the acid doesn't bubble or foam or generally react to the rock, it should be safe. Try to use rocks that match the substrate; in nature, rocks are just larger pieces of the substrate that haven't been worn down. Rocks that differ from the substrate can be used, even as focal points, but the overall effect may not be as natural.

After the substrate is in place, consider the water. This may be the most critical step in the success of the aquarium. What water should be used? That depends on the animals to be kept. Most of the species discussed here prefer water that is at least slightly acidic and relatively soft. Purchasing a broad-range pH kit and a general hardness kit will go a long way toward ensuring your success.

If your tap water is hard and alkaline, using it directly is probably not a good idea. There are a number of options in this situation. A reverse osmosis (RO) unit can be installed or the water can be run through a deionizing unit. With either of these options, some minerals must be added back to the water. There are commercial products designed for this purpose, or a small amount of tap water (5–10 percent) can be added. RO water can also be purchased rather than produced at home; grocery stores and mass marketers often sell it, and most pet shops do as well. Many bottled-water delivery companies offer RO water as an option, too, so you can have it delivered if carrying it home from the store is problematic. It's a good idea to test purchased RO water prior to use because not all shops change their membranes as often as they should.

Rainwater is also a viable option, but using it can be risky due to pollution and other factors. Rainwater must always be allowed to age and should be filtered with activated carbon or some other chemical filter media to help to remove any pollutants. While it is being aged and filtered, peat moss or beech, Indian almond, or oak leaves can be added to acidify and soften it, making it a good choice for blackwater species. Test the pH and hardness before adding it to the aquarium.

Naturally adjusting the water chemistry is preferable to adding buffers because it tends to be more stable. As mentioned above, a few leaves can be added to the tank to keep the chemistry where you want it to be. The use of buffers leads to the "pH rollercoaster" effect: the buffer is added and the pH goes down, then the buffer "wears off" and the pH goes up, so more buffer is added and the process repeats. This dramatic fluctuation is incredibly stressful for the inhabitants.

Now, it's time to add the water. Do this very slowly. It is a good idea to pour the water onto a small dish held above the aquarium water to avoid unduly disturbing the substrate. This will help to keep fine particulates in the substrate and maintain the water's clarity.

Fill the tank approximately two-thirds full of water and then plant your aquascape according to your drawing. Adding the plants in an orderly manner, for example back to front, is easier than planting them haphazardly. You can set the plants by hand or use tweezers or tongs. The key is to be as gentle as possible with the

Clown Killifish, Epiplatys annulatus, *prefers soft, acidic water in the pH range of 4.0–7.0 to encourage breeding and maintain good coloration.*

plants to avoid damaging them. Information on where and how to plant is included in the plant profiles.

After the planting is complete, fill the aquarium and turn on the filtration and lighting. Run the lights 24 hours per day for the first few days to help the plants acclimate to their new submersed home. Then put the lights on a timer. If you have more than one aquarium, the day length will vary a bit from tank to tank. The idea is to find the point at which we get the most plant growth and the least algae growth. Start by keeping the lights on for 10 hours a day and adjust up or down from there, based on your observations of the plants. The times at which the lights go on or off is not critical, so set them to be on when you will be observing the tank. The key is photoperiod, not start or end time.

Strategies for maintaining a small tank

Many people purchase a small aquarium with the thought that it will be easier to maintain than a larger tank or because they are attracted to the small amount of space required. The reality is that despite its small size, a nano-aquarium has its own set of challenges and can be more difficult to take care of because there is significantly less dilution and less margin for error. Due to this, proper maintenance is especially important. You can compensate for the difficulty in volume by decorating the aquarium naturally, having suitable filtration for your livestock, and using numerous plants.

Maintenance has its own set of obstacles, as the majority of inhabitants of a small tank are quite petite themselves and can be damaged by something as simple as a water siphon. In addition, many species have very specialized needs, so large fluctuations in water chemistry must be avoided. The best way to alleviate many issues is to make sure a tank is well cycled prior to adding its inhabitants. The addition of live plants greatly helps to stabilize the nitrogen cycle and provides a more natural environment for your fishes and invertebrates. They are also very useful as a food supplementation, as invertebrates will graze on their surfaces and many small fishes will nibble on the microorganisms they produce.

TEST KIT ESSENTIALS

When determining your nano plans, it is important to be know about the water you will be able to provide and choose the livestock accordingly. A test kit for testing hardness (gH and kH), as well as ammonia, nitrite, and nitrate, is essential and lets you know when your tank is ready for the addition of livestock. Adding established media from a previous tank (gravel, a dirty filter sponge, or plants and décor) can speed up the preparation time.

Once your tank is decorated and planted and your water chemistry remains stable (no detectable ammonia or nitrite, and low levels of nitrate), you can introduce the first inhabitants. It is important, especially in a small tank, to test the water frequently, as the majority of small fishes and invertebrates are very intolerant of unstable and damaging water quality. Due to the low water volume

Healthy plants, inverts, and fishes, such as the tiny Panda Loach—at center, perched on foliage—will result if you follow simple guidelines: do not overstock, feed carefully, and perform regular small water changes and maintenance.

in a small tank, it is very common to have large spikes in parameters. You should be prepared to do small frequent water changes, even daily, after the initial setup. Continuing to add cultures of beneficial bacteria for nitrification is recommended and can help dramatically reduce the stress associated with establishing the nitrogen cycle.

It is important to stock a new setup slowly, allowing time for the tank to regulate and adjust to the new inhabitants. During this time, it is also important to feed the fishes and invertebrates sparingly, to reduce the waste in the water.

Once your tank is established, weekly maintenance becomes appropriate. Regular water changes of about 30 percent are generally recommended, though more or less may be required depending on the stocking density and species. Again, because of the small volume, one must be aware of the buffering capacity of the water. Sometimes it is better to do smaller, more frequent changes to prevent large fluctuations. The plants in a nano-aquarium must be maintained, too. Fast-growing plants can quickly take over a nano-aquarium and must be pruned regularly. Remove dead leaves and plant matter. Continue to test your values about twice a week for the first few months. Once your tank readings become consistent, you can test monthly or after the addition of new livestock.

There are several important considerations for maintenance, including the choice of siphon. It is extremely important to maintain your substrate in a tank, and using a very small-diameter siphon, such as airline tubing, is generally the best way to do this.

It is also important to rinse filter media during weekly maintenance; shrimp, especially, are very sensitive to a buildup of organic material. By maintaining your substrate and filter media and doing weekly water changes, you can keep the water parameters in the ideal range. Another part of regular maintenance is to maintain the glass. Aquarists often choose to allow the algae and biofilm to thrive and grow on the backs and sides of the glass, just cleaning the front viewing portion of the tank. Many of the nano-species, especially snails and shrimp, rely on these biofilms and microorganisms for their health and a large part of their diet.

Another important consideration in nano-aquariums is temperature. Quite a few species are less tropical and more temperate, and nano-aquariums are prone to getting quite warm from just the provided lighting. It is important to pay attention to the temperature and decide on a heater accordingly. As water gets warmer, there is less dissolved oxygen available. Many nano-species originate in streams or bodies of water with a high oxygen content, so temperature and aeration must be adequately maintained. Sponge-based biological filtration is generally ideal in a nano-aquarium, unless it is a low-pH system, as it poses no risk to small fishes or shrimp and the versatility of the bubble count allows for a good exchange of oxygen.

Fertilization of plants is also important to maintain their health. There are a few things to be aware of when choosing fertilizers. Invertebrates are intolerant of any levels of copper, and many bottled fertilizers contain it as a trace element. Also, many fertilizer dosing strategies are based on overdosing for the plants' needs, specifically nitrate. With this strategy, larger-volume water changes are utilized to remove the unused, excess nutrients. In a small tank, this can lead to dangerous levels of organics and fluctuations in parameters. It is better to do smaller dosing initially, and then determine the plants' needs based on their growth and health. You may need to change the water more frequently than usual in order to maintain low nitrate levels. Carbon dioxide acts as a form of fertilizer and can help provide the plants with carbon, lower and stabilize the pH, and reduce excessive algae. There are several types of CO_2 systems: liquids containing carbon dioxide, homemade systems using yeast, and those using pressurized gas bottles, which are the best and easiest to regulate. It is extremely important to use a system that can be regulated to keep the tank stable.

As with any aquarium, it is important to familiarize youself with the needs of your livestock and be realistic in determining how much time you have to dedicate to maintaining your aquarium. Stock lightly if finding time for maintenance is an issue. Nowadays there are many different types of nano-aquariums available, as well as an amazing array of species of fishes, invertebrates, and plants, many of which are outlined in this book. Planning ahead by doing your research can make a nano-aquarium a very rewarding and beautiful experience for the both the aquarist and its inhabitants.

Aquarist and adventure traveler Steve Waldron's 4-gallon (15-L) home microcosm is filled with mossy Süsswassertang (Lomariopsis lineata) *and Dwarf Hairgrass* (Eleocharis parvula), *which shelter a colony of* Neoheterandia elegans *livebearers and* Neocaridina *dwarf shrimp.*

Meeting the nutritional needs of nano-animals

Feeding the inhabitants of a nano-aquarium can be a stressful endeavor for even the most focused of hobbyists. Tiny mouths, competition at multiple levels, and fears of predation are just a few of the concerns. With small creatures often have specialized feeding behaviors. We have fishes that are specialized grazers, eating only *aufwuchs* (microscopic algae and crustaceans found growing on rocks or substrate), fishes whose dietary needs require extremely small crustaceans, and fishes with such short digestive tracts that frequent feedings of protein and fat-rich foods are a necessity.

As the range of small fishes and invertebrates has grown, so has the list of suitable foods on the market. No longer is it absolutely necessary to culture all your own foods, because it is possible to buy gel diets, small frozen foods, and dried foods like *CYCLOP-EEZE®* and Golden Pearls that mimic live brine shrimp nauplii.

The new gel diets can supplement live and frozen foods. My *aufwuchs* grazers (*Stiphodon, Ancistrus, Otocinclus*, shrimp, and others) are fed a reconstituted gel diet, such as Repashy's Soilent Green. This very versatile diet can be applied to surfaces such as driftwood, rocks, or tiles in order to cater to the grazing preferences of the fishes. When you provide a food that is stable in the water column for a prolonged period of time, the fishes or invertebrates with long digestive tracts can graze at will, allowing for a more natural consumption of nutrients.

Many fishes in this guide are micropredators, and they do best when fed a rotating variety of meaty foods, live, frozen, or dry: newly hatched baby brine shrimp, *Cyclops, Daphnia,* and worms of various types, such as Microworms, Grindal worms, and rotifers. Feeding invertebrates can follow the same guidelines, though the addition of live plants is welcome. If they have access to live plants, the shrimp can graze constantly on the infusoria that grow on the plants' surfaces.

Another strategy for supplementing the feeding of small fishes is the addition of apple snails (*Pomacea diffusa*). They are plant safe and provide a source of paramecium, excreted through their waste along with poorly digested herbivorous material.

Chili Rasboras in a feeding frenzy brought on by a serving of Cyclops, *tiny crustaceans that are a staple for many micropredators.*

There are also many good prepared diets available, including pelleted and flake foods. It is important to know the needs of your inhabitants. Read the labels of prepared foods carefully. Primary ingredients listed should fulfill the requirements of your chosen tank inhabitants. For instance, for an algae-grazer some type of algae, such as *Spirulina*, should be among the first few ingredients, and a micropredator should be fed a food that lists some sort of crustacean as a primary ingredient.

One of the biggest dangers when feeding a nano-aquarium is overfeeding, which can lead to poor water quality and dramatic shifts in water chemistry—both of which can be lethal. Fishes with small mouths eat very little at one time, preferring small, frequent meals rather than one large feast. I try to fast the tank at least once a week, and then offer small meals tailored to the needs of specific species throughout the week.

Overfeeding can lead to secondary pests like *Planaria*, *Hydra*, and detritus worms in an aquarium. In a nano-tank, this can be especially dangerous to juvenile shrimp and even the smallest fishes. The use of feeding dishes (small terra cotta lids), slightly buried in the substrate, is recommended in invertebrate tanks. This allows for controlled placement of food and makes it easier to remove any uneaten food. It also prevents the wasted food from settling as readily within the substrate, where it can provide nutrition for potential pests and adversely affect water quality.

5.5-Gallon (20-L) Asian Rainforest Pool

9 Chili Rasbora	*Boraras brigittae*
1 Horned Nerite	*Clithon corona*
1 pair Flame Badis	*Dario hysginon*
8 Malawa Shrimp	*Caridina pareparensis parvidentata*

This will be a colorful and active tank with interest at all levels. Areas of dense planting utilizing mosses or *Riccia fluitans* will provide hiding places for the shrimp and help preserve their numbers from predation. There should be pieces of driftwood as well as some taller plants, which will help encourage the Flame Badis, *Dario hysginon*, to spawn. The Malawa Shrimp provide an added element of interest for the bottom of the biotope. —R.O.

5.5-Gallon (20-L) Colombian Blackwater Community

5 Green Neons	*Paracheirodon simulans*
3 Gold Tetras	*Hemigrammus rodwayi*
1 Oto	*Otocinclus* sp.
3 Dwarf Cory Cats	*Corydoras habrosus*

This is a small Colombian blackwater biotope community. The two small tetra species add color and movement and should spend most of their time at different water levels, with the Gold Tetras swimming above the Green Neons. (Common Neons could certainly be substituted.) In a true biotope, we'd only have leaf litter on the substrate and no plants, but we're going to modify it a bit. The plants should be mostly green, which will highlight the gold and the red of the tetras. Because we're including Dwarf Cory Cats, *Corydoras habrosus*, a significant portion of the bottom should be left open for swimming. Planting two species of stem plants along the back and maybe one side, with an interesting piece of driftwood as an off-center focal point, would work well. Slender Pondweed, *Potamogeton gayi*, is a South American native that could fit into this biotope. A thicket of it would make a nice contrast to a thicket of fine leaf Ambulia, *Mayaca fluviatilis*. Using these two species would contrast both leaf direction and shade of green. —M.D.

Flame Badis, Dario hysginon, *provide color and breeding action in nano scale.*

10-Gallon (38-L) Asian Valley Stream

9 Emerald Rasbora	*Danio erythromicron*
7 Rosy Loach	*Petruichthys* sp. "Rosy"
10 Yellow Shrimp	*Neocaridina davidi*
2 Nerite snails	*Neritina* sp.
3 Micro Crabs	*Limnopilos naiyanetri*

A well-planted tank with areas of open water is best for these inhabitants. The Rosy Loaches and danios will actively school together, utilizing the midwater of the tank. Floating plants or plants with obvious roots and a taller structure are recommended in order to increase the visibility of the crabs. Small pieces of wood or rock, as well as broad-leaved plants like *Anubias*, would provide good shelter for the crabs as well as a grazing surface for the snails. Some areas of dense planting utilizing *Sagittaria*, moss, or baby tears is recommended, as it will provide protective spaces for the eventual young shrimp. —*R.O.*

10-Gallon (38-L) Latin Festival Community

5 Red Flame Tetras	*Hyphessobrycon flammeus*
6 Pretty Tetras	*Hyphessobrycon pulcher*
or Head & Tail Light Tetras	*Hyphessobrycon ocellifer*
1 pair or trio Endler's Livebearer	*Poecilia wingei*
1 Clown Pleco	*Panaqolus maccus*
3 Panda Cory Cats	*Corydoras panda*

This group of fishes will be colorful and interesting in an aquarium but they are not found together in nature. Consequently, we're going to stray a bit afield when choosing plants for this aquascape. The tetras will look best under medium light, so the plants chosen should be able to do well with that constraint. We also need to leave some open swimming room for the Panda Cory Cats. Plant the back wall of the tank with Stream Bogmoss (*Mayaca fluviatilis*), which should cover it nicely and not take up a lot of bottom space. Plant a small group of chain swords in a front corner and small groups of two species of *Cryptocoryne* in the middle ground. The red leaves of *C. petchii* make it ideal as a focal point in this setup. Be sure to include a piece of driftwood for the Clown Pleco (*Panaqolus maccus*) to chew on. This will serve as the focal point in the other half of the tank. —*M.D.*

20-Gallon (76-L) South American Community

7 Rummynose Tetras	*Hemigrammus* or *Petitela* sp.
5 Lemon Tetras	*Hyphessobrycon pulchripinnis*
6 Coral Red Pencilfish	*Nannostomus morganthaleri*
1 pair Checkerboard Cichlids	*Dicrossus filamentosus*
or a pair of Rams	*Mikrogeophagus ramirezi*
1 pair Bristlenose Catfish	*Ancistrus* sp.

If you decide to add a pair of *Apistogrammas* to this community instead of the checkerboards or rams, be sure to add at least two Apisto caves so that they'll have somewhere to spawn if they want to and generally call home if they don't. Adding a couple of pleco caves will give the Bristlenose Plecos a place to spawn and hang out, too. All these ceramic caves are going to take up some bottom space, so planting should be limited. Small Anubias can be grown on the ceramic caves to help camouflage them. Any stem plants that do well in medium lighting can be planted along the back and sides. The interior should be planted with *Echinodorus* or *Cryptocoryne* species. The cichlids will appreciate a piece of driftwood, and a few rocks should be added if you put Rams in the tank, as they generally prefer to spawn on a hard substrate. —*M.D.*

Coral Red Pencilfish, excellent dither fish kept in groups with small cichlids.

41

LONG 20-Gallon (76-L) Asian Hillstream Community

1 pair Blue Neon Gobies	*Stiphodon atropurpureus*
3 Green Lace Shrimp	*Atyoida pilipes*
8 White Cloud Mountain Minnows	*Tanichthys albonubes*
7 Dwarf Zebra Hovering Loach	*Micronemacheilus cruciatus*
10 Red Cherry Shrimp	*Neocaridina davidi* (var. Red)
1 pair Scarlet Gobies	*Rhinogobius zhoui*

The shoals of loaches and White Clouds will utilize the middle of the tank, providing an extremely active and colorful display. The hillstream environment calls for oversized filtration and a directional powerhead to provide increased oxygenation and ample water flow. Décor should consist of pebbles and large rocks, stacked securely, to allow for many grazing sites for the *Stiphodons*. High lighting should be utilized to encourage algae growth, and most plants are unnecessary, although some Java Ferns or *Anubias* may be included for aesthetics. The varied and plentiful rockwork will provide spaces for the shrimp to hide, as well as ample areas for territory and displays of dominance by the different goby species. —R.O.

Cherry Shrimp in a colony of 10 or more will breed in this community.

HIGH 20-Gallon (76-L) Mixed Community

5 Marble Hatchetfish	*Carnegiella strigata*
6 Espe's Rasboras	*Trigonostigma espei*
7 Cardinal Tetras	*Paracheirodon axelrodi*
1 pair Honey Gouramis	*Trichogaster chuna*
3 Zebra Otos	*Otocinclus cocama*
5 Amano Shrimp	*Caridina multidentata*

I have used the combination of Marble Hatchets, Espe's Rasboras, and Cardinal Tetras in many, many planted aquariums over the years. This combination was almost a trademark for me when I was doing aquarium maintenance. These three species look great together and really work well due to their different colors and shapes and where they live in the water column. Adding a pair of Honey Gouramis that will cross all levels, along with the Zebra Otos and Amano Shrimp at the bottom, surely make this an aquarium most everyone will greatly enjoy. (I plant the Thai Lily, *Nyphmaea rubra*, for its lushness and bold color, but, as the species profile in this guide points out (page 154), it must be kept pruned so it can't put up pads and take over the tank.) —*M.D.*

Cardinal Tetras have a peaceful schooling nature.

Otocinclus suckermouth catfish, an ideal nano algae eater.

A field guide to nano-aquarium fishes, plants, and invertebrates

For the aquarium enthusiast, bringing home a new fish, invertebrate, or plant—one that you have never kept before and know only from reading about it and seeing it in your local aquarium shop's display tanks—is one of life's pulse-quickening moments.

To be sure that you are not bringing home a bag full of trouble or an organism that has little chance of surviving in a typical home aquarium, the following species are presented as great choices, especially for less experienced nano aquarists—or those who want to improve the odds that their new acquisitions will thrive.

For simplicity, the species are arranged in alphabetical order by common name of the family or group—Anabantoid (e.g. Betta), Catfish (e.g. Cory), Characin (e.g. Tetra)—and then by the scientific name of each species.

COLOR KEY TO SIZES

One of the most important criteria for selection of an aquarium specimen is its eventual adult size. Will it fit in your nano-aquarium? Will it be an appropriate tankmate for the fishes you have and/or plan to buy? That cute baby Oscar that fits into a 5-gallon nano for a while, but then grows into a greedy, foot-long predator that eats all your prized tetras and ornamental shrimp is probably not the best choice. Species that can be kept in small nano tanks can of course be kept in larger tanks as well.

Here is the Size Key used in this guide:

SMALL NANO:
Suitable for aquariums of 5 gallons (19 L) or less

MEDIUM NANO:
Suitable for aquariums of 6 to 10 gallons (23 to 38 L)

LARGE NANO:
Suitable for aquariums of 11 to 20 gallons (42 to 76 L)

JUST ADD FISH: Like a garden without birds or butterflies, a beautiful nano aquarium needs movement to complete a scene reflecting nature.

WINE RED BETTA *Betta coccina*
(Claret Betta, Scarlet Betta)

OVERVIEW: The type species of the *coccina* species complex, collectively known as the dwarf red fighters. Males are more colorful than females and have longer, more pointed dorsal and anal fins. There is some geographic variation in these wild bettas; some males feature a small metallic blue-green spot on the mid-body while those from other locations feature this color suffused throughout the body. One location has extended central caudal fin rays known as lancet fin. These variations may indicate multiple species. Fish from different locations should not be kept together to avoid unintended hybridization. The male builds a submersed bubble nest and cares for the eggs and fry until they are free-swimming.

NATIVE RANGE: peninsular Malaysia and the island of Sumatra

MAXIMUM SIZE: 1.6 inches (4 cm)

MINIMUM AQUARIUM SIZE: 2.5 gallons (10 liters)

WATER PARAMETERS: pH 4.0–7.5, soft water, 72–80°F

FEEDING: High quality flakes and pellets with frozen foods and live foods such as mosquito larvae, *Daphnia*, *Cyclops* and Grindal worms.

BEHAVIOR & CARE: Males will engage in mock battles but damage rarely ensues. Can be kept in a group in very small tanks. These bettas are very shy, and providing lots of hiding places is a necessity. Tankmates should be peaceful and not overly active. Keeping them with a school of small, peaceful fish such as a *Boraras* species will help them to overcome their shyness.

SIAMESE FIGHTING FISH *Betta splendens*
(Betta)

OVERVIEW: One of the most popular aquarium fishes, available in a range of colors and finnage varieties. This highly bred fish is actually a hybrid including most of the members of the *Splendens* species complex. Available forms include "plakat," with short, heavy fins, strong scales, and a muscular body; "half moon," featuring a 180-degree spread of the caudal fin; "double tail," with two caudal fins; "crowntail," with extended rays of the unpaired fins; and a host of others. Colors range throughout the rainbow and include solid colors and patterns ranging from pastel to metallic. The male builds a bubble nest and cares for the eggs and fry until they are free-swimming.

NATIVE RANGE: Thailand

MAXIMUM SIZE: 3 in. (8 cm) typical; giant form up to 6 in. (16 cm)

MINIMUM AQUARIUM SIZE: 1 gal. (4 L)

WATER PARAMETERS: pH 6.5–7.5, 70–85°F (21–29°C)

FEEDING: High quality flakes and pellets supplemented with frozen foods and live foods such as mosquito larvae, *Daphnia*, *Cyclops*, and Grindal worms.

BEHAVIOR & CARE: Males must be kept singly; females can be kept in groups. Males and females should only be together for spawning. Its long fins and slow swimming make it an easy target for fin-nippers. Males will attack fishes with large fins, like fancy guppies. Will nip at snails and shrimp. Best kept with peaceful species in a tank with moderate water flow.

SCARLET BADIS *Dario dario*
(Scarlet Gem Badis)

OVERVIEW: One of the most well-known badids in the aquarium hobby, they are staggeringly beautiful when in breeding dress. *Dario dario* is an excellent choice for the advanced hobbyist who has a small, heavily planted aquarium. They form temporary pair bonds and spawn like cichlids, depositing eggs on substrate—a leaf or in a cave.

NATIVE RANGE: India

MAXIMUM SIZE: 0.5–0.7 in. (1.3–1.8 cm)

MINIMUM AQUARIUM SIZE: 10 gal. (38 L)

WATER PARAMETERS: pH 6.5–8.5, 65–78°F (18–26°C)

FEEDING: Micropredator. Sometimes difficult to feed, Darios should be offered live foods as often as possible to get them into breeding condition. Live baby brine shrimp, white worms, or micro-worms are best; supplement with small frozen foods like *Cyclops* or *Daphnia*.

BEHAVIOR & CARE: While males are most prevalent in the hobby, if you can find females—which are significantly less colorful and have shorter pelvic fins—they are an excellent choice for a spawning project. Areas of dense planting and the addition of several cave-like structures help diffuse any male-on-male aggression and allow them to establish small territories that they will utilize in spawning. For best breeding success, they should be kept in a species tank, though they are compatible with other small, peaceful fishes. Dwarf shrimp housed in the same tank can offer them a ready supply of live food, as the adult shrimp are largely left alone.

RED FLAME DARIO *Dario hysginon*
(*Dario* sp. Myanmar, *D.* sp. Pyjamas, *D.* sp. Fire-Red Badis)

OVERVIEW: Gaining popularity due to their recent consistent availability, these rival *Dario dario* in vibrancy of color and beauty. Both commonly available and easier to feed, they are an excellent choice for hobbyists interested in a breeding project.

NATIVE RANGE: Myanmar

MAXIMUM SIZE: 0.7 in. (1.8 cm)

MINIMUM AQUARIUM SIZE: 5 gal. (19 L)

WATER PARAMETERS: pH 6.5–7.5, 59–78°F (15–26°C)

FEEDING: Micropredator. Difficult to supplement with dried foods. Live baby brine shrimp, white worms, or micro-worms are best, with supplementation of small frozen foods like *Cyclops* or *Daphnia*. This species will often accept fine flake foods as well.

BEHAVIOR & CARE: Care is similar to that of other small darios in that ample planting and cavelike structures should be provided in order to break up the line of sight and prevent aggression between males. Females of this species are much easier to obtain, and they are readily capable of being spawned. Pairs or trios are best, in a species tank for breeding or alongside other small, peaceful species like *Boraras*, *Microdevario*, or *Petruichthys* loaches. One should avoid keeping them with boisterous tankmates like danios, as they are easily out-competed for food. This fish is considered rare and its conservation status is threatened, so focus should be placed on captive breeding.

ORNATE BUSHFISH *Microctenopoma ansorgii*
(Ornate Climbing Perch)

OVERVIEW: This most colorful of the African labyrinth fishes typically inhabits overgrown areas near the banks of small streams. It is a bubblenest builder. Males are somewhat more colorful and have longer, more pointed dorsal and anal fins. In full courtship mode the male takes on glorious coloration. Something of a rarity and best reserved for experienced fishkeepers.

NATIVE RANGE: Congo River basin

MAXIMUM SIZE: 3 in. (8 cm)

MINIMUM AQUARIUM SIZE: 10 gal. (38 L)

WATER PARAMETERS: pH 6.0–7.5, moderately hard, 74–82°F (23-28°C)

FEEDING: Carnivore. Diet should consist primarily of live and frozen foods supplemented with high-protein flakes and pellets. Regular feeding of *Cyclops*, which are rich in carotenoids, encourages bright colors.

BEHAVIOR & CARE: Fares best in dimly lit aquariums decorated with driftwood and low-light plants. This shy species needs to have plenty of hiding places to feel secure or it will spend all its time hiding. The male's colors intensify during spawning, making it truly spectacular. Good tankmates include peaceful, schooling species that are too large to be eaten. Cardinal Tetras are an excellent choice, as are other similarly sized tetras and pencilfishes, the *Trigonostigma* species, and many of the rasboras. Small loaches, loricariids, and Corydoradinae catfishes also work well.

LICORICE GOURAMI *Parosphromenus* spp.

OVERVIEW: Licorice gouramis are are highly desirable and worthwhile subjects for advanced hobbyists. They require extremely soft, acidic water and a consistent diet of live foods. There are a number of species that are available occasionally, though most are misidentified. They are all blackwater species and aquarium water chemistry must simulate their natural habitat. *Parosphromenus quindecim* is shown above.

NATIVE RANGE: Malaysia, Borneo, Sumatra, Java

MAXIMUM SIZE: Varies by species, generally 1.5 in. (4 cm)

MINIMUM AQUARIUM SIZE: 5 gal. (19 L)

WATER PARAMETERS: pH 4-6.5, very soft, 70–75°F (21–24°C)

FEEDING: Micropredator. Feed tiny live foods only, with as much variation as possible. Some good choices include baby *Artemia*, vinegar eels, micro-worms, *Daphnia*, *Cyclops*, and wingless fruit flies.

BEHAVIOR & CARE: Licorice gouramis are shy and best kept in dedicated species tanks or with a school of very small, very peaceful fishes. Small shrimp can also be good tankmates, and the licorice gouramis may eat a few of the shrimplets. Licorice gouramis spend much of their time in leaf litter, feeding on microfauna and hiding from predators. The addition of Indian Almond (*Catappa*), beech, or oak leaves is much appreciated. The décor should also include some driftwood and plants. Most species build submersed bubble nests. Licorice gouramis should only be acquired after researching the species and preparing the aquarium. Additional information is available online from the Parosphromenus Project at http://parosphromenus-project.org/en/.

SAMURAI CHOCOLATE GOURAMI *Sphaerichthys vaillanti*
(Vaillant's Chocolate Gourami)

OVERVIEW: The easiest chocolate gourami to maintain as well as the most colorful. That said, the species is still somewhat delicate and is prone to shipping stress, sometimes resulting in an infestation of velvet. Suitable for hobbyists with some experience, it is not as demanding as the other members of the genus in terms of diet or water chemistry. Females are larger and more colorful than males. Paternal mouthbrooder. The female guards the male while he broods the eggs and fry. In wild fish, only the dominant female will develop full coloration. In captive bred fish, the males will sometimes show the same color pattern as the females.

NATIVE RANGE: Borneo

MAXIMUM SIZE: 1.7 in.

MINIMUM AQUARIUM SIZE: 5 gallons for a pair or 10 gallons in a community setting

WATER PARAMETERS: 5–7, soft, 72–80°F

FEEDING: Carnivore. Feed a varied diet including dry and frozen foods. Live foods should make up a significant portion of the diet.

BEHAVIOR & CARE: The male coloration combined with their mode of swimming mimics a dead leaf. A biotope that features driftwood and plants with low to moderate lighting is ideal. Small peaceful tankmates such as *Boraras* or *Paracheirodon* species look good with them and will help to make them feel more secure so that they will be more active.

HONEY DWARF GOURAMI *Trichogaster chuna*
(Honey Gourami)

OVERVIEW: The most peaceful member of the genus. Males display their best coloration when in spawning condition, but that color is worth the wait, as in the image above. Several captive-bred morphs are available, but their colors are drab compared to the wild male's breeding dress. Honey Gouramis are usually found in slow-flowing waters that flood seasonally, leading to wide fluctuations in water chemistry. The male builds a bubblenest to incubate the eggs.

NATIVE RANGE: India, Bangladesh

MAXIMUM SIZE: 2.25 in. (6 cm)

MINIMUM AQUARIUM SIZE: 10 gal. (38 L)

WATER PARAMETERS: pH 6–8, soft to hard, 74–80°F (23–27°C)

FEEDING: Omnivore. They accept everything the hobbyist offers, so it is easy to fall into the habit of feeding dry food, but the chances for long-term success are much greater with frozen and live foods. Frozen *Cyclops*, *Daphnia*, and *Mysis* shrimp are good high-protein foods. Wingless fruit flies are a real treat and can be gut-loaded with *Spirulina* powder and NatuRose (a natural astaxanthin pigment supplement) mashed into over-ripe banana prior to being fed to the fish.

BEHAVIOR & CARE: Honey Gouramis seem happiest when maintained in a group. There will be a dominance hierarchy, but actual damage is seldom inflicted. Dimly lit tanks with lots of hiding places suit them best. Peaceful schooling species like *Boraras* help them feel secure enough to spend most of their time in the open. Small catfishes or loaches are good additions to the lower levels of the tank.

DWARF GOURAMI *Trichogaster lalius*
(Formerly *Colisa lalia*)

OVERVIEW: One of the most common labyrinth fishes in the hobby. Wild fish are occasionally available from India, but almost all the fish sold are commercially bred. Selective breeding has resulted in numerous color forms, including the fire or flame, neon dwarf and rainbow dwarf. Males are significantly more colorful, so they are most often offered for sale. Finding females can sometimes be a challenge.

NATIVE RANGE: Pakistan, India, Bangladesh

MAXIMUM SIZE: 3 in. (8 cm)

MINIMUM AQUARIUM SIZE: 10 gal. (38 L)

WATER PARAMETERS: pH not critical, 74–82°F (23–28°C)

FEEDING: Omnivore. Offer foods made for carnivores as well as those made for herbivores. Frozen and live foods are generally taken with gusto.

BEHAVIOR & CARE: Quarantine is an absolute necessity with this species, which is prone to and frequently carrying the Dwarf Gourami Iridovirus (DGIV). Most specimens have gill flukes, so treat for them in quarantine. Left untreated, gill flukes weaken a fish so that it becomes susceptible to secondary infections. After quarantine, add to a well-planted aquarium with relatively low water movement. If spawning is desired, add some floating plants to provide a place to anchor the nest. This gourami has been known to rid aquariums of beard algae infestations by using the algae in bubble-nest construction. Does well with most rasboras and tetras.

SPARKLING GOURAMI *Trichopsis pumila*
(Pygmy Gourami)

OVERVIEW: The *Trichopsis* species are essentially aquatic crickets, producing croaking sounds by rapidly beating their pectoral fins. The sound is used in displays that determine dominance and position within the social hierarchy, as well as to attract a mate. Despite being the smallest fish in the genus, *T. pumila* makes the loudest sounds. Its diminutive size makes the Sparkling Gourami the best of the genus for inclusion in nano-tanks.

NATIVE RANGE: Vietnam, Thailand, Laos, Cambodia, peninsular Malaysia, and the Islands of Borneo and Sumatra

MAXIMUM SIZE: 1.5 in. (4 cm)

MINIMUM AQUARIUM SIZE: 10 gal. (38 L)

WATER PARAMETERS: Native to blackwater environments but adapts to a wide range of water conditions, 76–82°F (24–28°C).

FEEDING: Omnivore. Almost any food will be readily accepted, but be sure to include some frozen and live foods in the diet.

BEHAVIOR & CARE: Sparkling Gouramis are somewhat shy and retiring. Their colors show best in moderately lit planted aquariums. Some driftwood should be added to provide hiding places. The presence of a school of small, peaceful fishes, such as one of the *Boraras*, *Trigonostigma*, or *Laubuca* species, will serve as an early warning system for the gouramis and encourage them to spend more time in view. Bottom-dwelling tankmates should also be added, and *Hara* catfish, the various loaches, and the smaller Corydoradinae or loricariids all do well with them.

ASIAN HILLSTREAM CATFISHES *Akysis* spp.
(Wasp Catfish, Stone Catfish, Micro Bumblebee Catfish)

OVERVIEW: *Akysis* is a genus with several minute species of Asian stream catfishes, including *Akysis vespa* and others. They are uncommon in the aquarium trade but adorable, with orange and black patterning. They are not difficult to keep, but should be offered plenty of hiding places, as they enjoy squeezing into crevices and burying in sand. There are several species within the genus that are commonly confused with *Akysis vespa*, many of which get larger at maturity (up to 2 inches/5 cm). The patterning on *Akysis vespa* is generally much broader than on others, and the caudal fin has equally sized lobes.

NATIVE RANGE: Upper reaches of the Ataran River drainage in south Myanmar.

MAXIMUM SIZE: 1.2 in. (3 cm)

MINIMUM AQUARIUM SIZE: 5 gal. (19 L)

WATER PARAMETERS: pH 6-7.5, 60-75°F (16-24°C)

FEEDING: Nocturnal micropredator. Readily accepts small frozen foods like *Daphnia*, bloodworms, and most small, meaty pellets.

BEHAVIOR & CARE: Not especially competitive, so it should be paired with dwarf schooling species like *Boraras*, *Microdevario*, and small danios or rasboras. Other appropriate tankmates include small tetras, livebearers, and loaches. Impeccable water quality is required, as these species originate in fast-moving, clear waters. Can be kept singly or in a group, as they are not aggressive toward conspecifics. While nocturnal, they are energetic and exciting when being fed.

GREEN DRAGON ANCISTRUS *Ancistrus* cf. *cirrhosus*
(Common Bristlenose, Bushy Nose Pleco)

OVERVIEW: The Green Dragon is just one of many color forms of the Common Bristlenose Pleco. Widely available in its natural brown, albino, and often even in a red or calico pattern, the Bristlenose Pleco is one of the most popular loricariids kept in the hobby. Easy to breed and maintain, they are a wonderful addition to any community planted tank. Ancistrus catfishes make wonderful components of an authentic Amazonian biotope.

NATIVE RANGE: South America, most domestically bred

MAXIMUM SIZE: 4.9 in. (12 cm)

MINIMUM AQUARIUM SIZE: 10 gal. (38 L)

WATER PARAMETERS: pH 5.8–7.6, 70–80°F (21–27°C)

FEEDING: Herbivorous grazer. They should be fed *Spirulina* wafers and a range of blanched vegetables, such as zucchini and sweet potato. Wood is important for them to graze upon. They do enjoy the occasional treat of meaty pellets or frozen foods. Gelatinized foods are a good choice for this grazer.

BEHAVIOR & CARE: Easy to sex, as the male develops prominent bristles on its head and the female does not. They are easy to breed if ceramic caves, areas of stacked wood, or PVC pipe are provided. The male traps the female in the cave and then guards the eggs until the fry are free-swimming. This is a gentle and unassuming fish, and can be kept in a community tank with the smallest and most timid fishes. There is much confusion about the actual species because so many unidentified congeners exist.

ALBATER CORY CAT *Aspidoras albater*
(False Micropterus)

OVERVIEW: The charming little catfishes classified in the genus *Aspidoras* are very much like their close relatives in the genus *Corydoras*. Several species are becoming more available among hobbyists, including *A. albater, A. pauciradiatus, A. spilotus, A. poecilus,* and the unidentified *Aspidoras* sp. C 35 "Black Phantom." These are some of the best catfishes for the nano-aquarium, active but completely unaggressive. Females are larger and more robust than males.

NATIVE RANGE: Rio Tocantins, Brazil

MAXIMUM SIZE: 1.8 in. (4.5 cm)

MINIMUM AQUARIUM SIZE: 5 gal. (19 L)

WATER PARAMETERS: pH 6–7.5, soft to moderately hard, 72–76°F (22–24°C)

FEEDING: Micropredator. Feed dry foods designed for catfishes plus frozen and live foods. *Aspidorus* catfishes are particularly fond of worms and baby brine shrimp.

BEHAVIOR & CARE: These bottom-dwelling cats are surprisingly good jumpers, so a tight-fitting cover is recommended. Completely peaceful, it does best in a school of at least six fish. Add to a planted aquarium with some driftwood for cover. Leave an open area at the front of the tank for swimming and digging in the substrate, which should be fine and smooth so that it doesn't cut the fish's sensitive barbels. In good conditions, they will spawn in the aquarium, and a few fry may survive in an established, heavily planted tank.

RETICULATED DRIFTWOOD CAT *Centromochlus reticulatus*
(Synonymous with *Tatia reticulata*)

OVERVIEW: A striking little nocturnal catfish, this species is more outgoing than most others in the genus, actively feeding off the surface of the tank. With its purple color and honeycomb patterning, this is arguably one of the most attractive of the wood cats.

NATIVE RANGE: Guyana, Peru, Brazil

MAXIMUM SIZE: 1.2 in. (3 cm)

MINIMUM AQUARIUM SIZE: 10 gal. (38 L) for a group

WATER PARAMETERS: pH 6-7.5, 70-78°F (21-26°C)

FEEDING: Micropredator. Offer a steady diet of bloodworms or white worms. Do not feed many crustaceans.

BEHAVIOR & CARE: Like others in the genus, this species appreciates a dim tank with a jumble of driftwood or ceramic caves. They squeeze into crevices, usually appearing only during their very active feeding time. Adding a powerhead for strong directional flow is advised, as they appreciate the current. They can be spawned. The male has a modified and elongated anal fin which resembles a gonopodium and is used for internal fertilization. Females are generally slightly smaller and much wider-bodied. The males are more active in the tank, often swimming midwater or at the surface, seeking out the more elusive females. While most plants won't do well in the dim setting, *Anubias* planted so that it nears the water's surface makes an ideal place for them to lay their eggs. To induce spawning, feed live or frozen worms in small, frequent feedings, and cease water changes. Remove or reduce light on the tank. The females get noticeably rotund when they are about to lay their eggs.

SALT AND PEPPER CORY CAT *Corydoras habrosus*
(Dainty Cory, Venezuelan Pygmy Cory)

OVERVIEW: This is the smallest bottom-oriented member of the genus. While they will eat most food that reaches the substrate, it is important to meet their nutritional needs to ensure their continued health and well-being. They do not eat fish feces and should be added to an aquarium for their looks and interesting behavior, not as a clean-up crew. Almost all *C. habrosus* in the aquarium trade are wild-collected, so they are seasonally available. Some years they are not plentiful or are not in good condition, while other years they are very common and seem to do very well. If you don't succeed with this species the first time, try them again the following year.

NATIVE RANGE: Colombia, Venezuela

MAXIMUM SIZE: 1.4 in. (3.5 cm)

MINIMUM AQUARIUM SIZE: 5 gal. (19 L)

WATER PARAMETERS: pH 6.5–7.5, 70–78°F (21–26°C)

FEEDING: Micropredator. Uses its sensitive barbels to find food organisms on or in the substrate. Feed pellets designed for catfishes and high quality flakes for omnivores. Supplement dry food with frozen foods. Adding live foods, like baby brine shrimp and black, tropical red, or Grindal worms, helps to bring them into spawning condition.

BEHAVIOR & CARE: This sociable species does best when kept in a school of five or more individuals. The aquarium should be planted and decorated with driftwood and/or rocks to provide hiding places. Leave a large open area of soft substrate where they can spend their time.

PANDA CORY *Corydoras panda*
(Panda Catfish)

OVERVIEW: This eye-catching little cat was an instant hit when first imported, and it has earned a reputation as one of the most popular and well-liked catfishes in the hobby. With the typical wiggly and exuberant behavior of most *Corydoras* and the striking contrast in patterning, this fish is suitable for all levels of hobbyist and an excellent choice for a nano–community tank.

NATIVE RANGE: South America, upper Amazon drainage in Peru

MAXIMUM LENGTH: 2.5 in (6 cm)

MINIMUM AQUARIUM SIZE: 15 gal. (95 L)

WATER: pH 6.5–7.5, hardness 0–20°dGH, 70–79°F (21–26°C)

FEEDING: Micropredator. Readily accepts any sinking meaty foods or live foods. Feed pellets designed for catfishes and high quality flakes for omnivores. Supplement dry food with frozen foods. The addition of live foods such as baby *Artemia* and black, tropical red, or Grindal worms helps to bring them into spawning condition.

BEHAVIOR & CARE: These little cats will show their best colors against a light substrate; if dark sand or gravel is used they will darken to improve their camouflage. They are easy to breed, even by novices, and will often spawn in a community tank without any assistance from the aquarist. Very peaceful and suitable for most community tanks, but do not keep it with anything large or aggressive. The best tankmates include small characins, cyprinids, anabantoids, dwarf cichlids, and other peaceful catfishes. As a schooling species, they are best maintained in groups of six or more.

PYGMY CORY *Corydoras pygmaeus*
(Pygmy Catfish)

OVERVIEW: One of the most readily available of the dwarf cory species, pygmy cories are a popular choice for a small tank and excellent tankmates for other small and peaceful fishes and invertebrates, including small, vulnerable shrimp species. Versatile and easy to feed, when in large groups they spend much of their time utilizing the entire tank, swimming mid-water in tight schools and making use of décor like driftwood and *Anubias* to rest. It lives in groups in nature, and more is better, making them increasingly outgoing as the group gains in size.

NATIVE RANGE: Brazil, Colombia, Peru

MAXIMUM SIZE: 1.2 in. (3 cm)

MINIMUM AQUARIUM SIZE: 5 gal. (19 L)

WATER PARAMETERS: pH 6.4–7.5, 72–79°F (22–26°C)

FEEDING: Micropredator. It will readily accept meaty pellets, but thrives when offered live worms or frozen baby brine shrimp, *Daphnia*, or *Cyclops*.

BEHAVIOR & CARE: Petite and undemanding, this species is perfect for an Amazon biotope tank. It is suitable to keep with species like *Apistogramma*, most small characins, cyprinids, and dwarf shrimp. One should avoid keeping them with larger catfishes, angelfishes, and gouramis. They are facultative air breathers, so especially deep tanks should be avoided. This fish is often confused with *C. hastatus*, which has a black diamond-shaped spot at the caudal peduncle and is very difficult to source.

ASIAN STONE CATFISH *Hara jerdoni*
(Mini-Moth Catfish, Anchor Catfish, Dwarf Moth Catfish)

OVERVIEW: Tiny and unassuming, this little catfish can add a unique level of interest to the bottom of a tank. It is found in the wild in slow-moving hillstreams in the Ganges-Brahmaputra River drainages east to Thailand, and is a perfect addition to an Asian stream biotope. It can and should be maintained in groups for its own sense of security and to offer the aquarist opportunities to observe its social behaviors. It tends to be shy, but will be bolder in the presence of others of its own species.

NATIVE RANGE: India, Bangladesh

MAXIMUM SIZE: 1.2 in. (3 cm)

MINIMUM AQUARIUM SIZE: 2 gal. (8 L)

WATER PARAMETERS: pH 5.6–7.6, 64–75°F (18–24°C)

FEEDING: Micropredator. Offer a variety of live, frozen, and high quality dry foods; white worms, baby brine shrimp, *Cyclops,* and *Daphnia*. May be offered small, meaty pellets.

BEHAVIOR & CARE: Because of its shy nature, *Hara jerdoni* should not be housed with other bottom-dwelling species, as it is easily out-competed for food. Appropriate tankmates include darios and danios and any of the small rasboras. One should avoid keeping it with any boisterous species, as its already shy nature will be compounded. It should be in a tank with a sandy substrate and both plants and driftwood where it can find refuge. It has been bred in the aquarium.

ORANGE ZEBRA OTO *Hypoptopoma* sp. *"Peru"*
(Robocop Catfish)

OVERVIEW: One of the smallest *Hypoptopoma*, this flashy little fish is an excellent choice for a mature, well-planted small aquarium. With a distinctive red ring around its eye and the orange and zebra-patterned body, it is extremely popular with advanced hobbyists, albeit uncommon to find.

NATIVE RANGE: Alto Nanay, Peru

MAXIMUM SIZE: 1.2 in. (3 cm)

MINIMUM AQUARIUM SIZE: 5 gal. (19 L)

WATER PARAMETERS: pH 6–7.5, 72–80°F (22–27°C)

FEEDING: Herbivorous grazer. Specialized gelatinized diets are the ideal supplementation, along with high quality *Spirulina* or vegetable-based pellets. An obligate grazer, it should be housed in a tank containing some driftwood.

BEHAVIOR & CARE: While relatively unassuming in care, clean water is a necessity. It is important to be sure that the aquarium is well established, as this grazer's diet can be difficult to supplement. Caution should be taken not to house this fish with other loricariids that may out-compete it for food. Appropriate tankmates are schooling species of comparable size like *Hyphessobrycons*, *Boraras*, *Trigonostigma*, and dwarf *Corydoras*. It is an ideal tankmate for dwarf shrimp and other invertebrates, as it will not predate on young shrimp. *Hypoptopoma* are distinguished by their stocky bodies and wide, flattened heads, which have a concave profile, and their thin tails.

OTO *Otocinclus vittatus*
(Dwarf Algae Eater, Dwarf Suckerfish)

OVERVIEW: Otos are exceptionally common and are inexpensively available in just about every aquarium fish store in the world. They have delicate mouths and an appetite for soft algae, so they are wonderful as a maintenance crew in a planted community tank. They are schooling fish, so they should be kept in groups of at least six; ten or more is ideal.

NATIVE RANGE: Colombia

MAXIMUM SIZE: 1.8 in. (4.6 cm)

MINIMUM AQUARIUM SIZE: 10 gal. (38 L)

WATER PARAMETERS: pH 6–7.5, 70–78°F (21–26°C)

FEEDING: Herbivorous grazers. Specialized gelatinized foods are best. Driftwood and leaf litter can be added for them to graze on, and plants are preferred as a source of biofilm, which they will also busily clean.

BEHAVIOR & CARE: This species thrives in a densely planted aquarium with roots, twigs, or branches. Many species are imported into the pet trade and they can be very difficult to differentiate, though the care of all is identical. Immaculate water quality and a well-established tank are necessary, as they are very difficult to supplement with dried foods. One should avoid keeping them with fishes that have large mouths, because they have spines that can become embedded in a predator's oral cavity, often proving fatal to both fishes. They complement dwarf shrimps and any small, peaceful fishes.

ZEBRA OTO *Otocinclus cocama*
(Tiger Oto)

OVERVIEW: This stunning algae-eater is a great addition to an invertebrate or peaceful community tank. Because of their modified dentition, they are easier to supplement than many algae-eaters, and are strikingly vivid in a planted aquarium. Social by nature, they do best in groups of six or more individuals.

NATIVE RANGE: Peru

MAXIMUM SIZE: 1.8 in. (4.6 cm)

MINIMUM AQUARIUM SIZE: 10 gal. (38 L)

WATER PARAMETERS: pH 6–7.5, 70–78°F (21–26°C)

FEEDING: Zebra Otos, like their more common relative, are herbivorous grazers. Pellets consisting of largely algae or herbivorous matter, as well as specialized gelatinized foods, are best. Driftwood and leaf litter can be added for them to graze on, and plants are preferred as a source of biofilms, which they will remove with their suctioning mouths.

BEHAVIOR & CARE: Despite their often hefty price tag, this species is well suited for community tanks and planted aquariums. *Otocinclus* are often fragile and thin upon import, so a lengthy quarantine procedure should be observed. They can be housed with diminutive, non-aggressive characids, smaller callichthyid or loricariid catfishes, and freshwater shrimp from the genera *Caridina* or *Neocaridina*. This species thrives in a densely planted aquarium with roots, twigs, or branches.

CLOWN PANAQUE *Panaqolus maccus*
(Clown Pleco, LDA022, L104, L162, Ringlet Pleco)

OVERVIEW: *Panaqolus maccus* is one of the most popular and common species of small striped loricariid in the hobby. ("Maccus" is from the Latin for buffoon or clown.) It is widely available and compatible with most common community aquarium fishes. They are grazers on wood and vegetation, and the tank should contain wood, which forms a large part of their diet.

NATIVE RANGE: Venezuela, Colombia

MAXIMUM SIZE: 3.9 in. (10 cm)

MINIMUM AQUARIUM SIZE: 10 gal. (38 L)

WATER PARAMETERS: pH 6.8–7.6, 73–82°F (23–28°C)

FEEDING: This is a wood-eating fish, and there should be ample types of driftwood in the tank. They can be supplemented with blanched vegetables like zucchini, cucumber, and sweet potato, as well as meaty frozen foods on occasion.

BEHAVIOR & CARE: A peaceful fish that is well suited to the community tank, provided it contains driftwood. The tank needs good mechanical filtration, as these fish produce a lot of waste from their diet of driftwood. They do well with other loricariids, small tetras, hatchets, and dwarf cichlids. One should avoid keeping them with too many other grazing species unless heavy filtration is provided. For detailed information on their breeding, including mimicking a dry season to initiate spawning, see www.PlanetCatfish.com, an excellent online reference for facts and trivia about aquarium catfishes.

UPSIDE-DOWN CATFISH *Synodontis nigriventris*

OVERVIEW: This unusual African species from Zaire spends most of its time upside down. It prefers to hang out under driftwood or in rock caves, where it keeps its belly oriented to the solid surface. Fairly nocturnal, Upside-Down Cats will come out to feed once they are fully acclimated to their surroundings. Potentially reaching 4 inches in length, they seldom exceed 2.5 inches, so they are a good choice for a nano-aquarium as long as their tankmates are carefully chosen.

NATIVE RANGE: Middle Congo River basin including Malebo Pool, formerly known as Stanley Pool

MAXIMUM SIZE: 4 in. (10 cm)

MINIMUM AQUARIUM SIZE: 15 gal. (57 L)

WATER PARAMETERS: pH 6–8, moderate to hard, 72–80°F (22–27°C)

FEEDING: Omnivore. Upside-Down Cats will eat almost any food offered and will take floating food from the surface while in an inverted position. Be sure to include some live food in the diet. Tropical redworms are particularly relished.

BEHAVIOR & CARE: This species is more likely to come out to play in a dimly lit tank. The importance of caves and driftwood cannot be overstated. This is a social species that can be kept in a group in larger aquariums but is probably best as a single fish in a small nano-tank. Be sure that any potential tankmates are large enough not to become snacks, and everyone should get along well. Females are larger than males.

RUBY TETRA *Axelrodia riesei*

OVERVIEW: Ruby Tetras are exceptionally petite and very striking, with a rich red color when in good condition. Aquarium-kept specimens like those shown above may lose their red hue, but are still very attractive. Imported specimens are often thin and require nurturing to encourage the rich red color for which they are known. Planted tanks with natural leaf litter are best, as these fish are said to come from areas of blackwater.

NATIVE RANGE: Colombia

MAXIMUM SIZE: 0.8 in. (2 cm)

MINIMUM AQUARIUM SIZE: 5 gal. (19 L)

WATER PARAMETERS: pH 4–6.5, 72–82°F (22–28°C)

FEEDING: Micropredator. Small, frequent feedings of live or frozen foods like baby brine shrimp, white worms, or *Daphnia* are best. May take some very small dried foods, like micro-pellets or flake. Offer pigment-enhancing dried specialty foods and *Cyclops* (frozen or dry CYCLOP-EEZE®) to help retain or restore their natural red coloration.

BEHAVIOR & CARE: Groups of 10 or more of this tiny species are recommended. They are shoaling more than schooling, and males set up small territories, which they defend. Because of their small stature, caution should be taken with pairing them with many fishes from similar areas. They do well with *Otocinclus* or dwarf *Corydoras* or in a species-specific tank. Boisterous tankmates should be avoided. Would-be shrimp breeders take note: they will eat baby ornamental crustaceans.

MARBLED HATCHETFISH *Carnegiella strigata*
(Marbled Hatchet)

OVERVIEW: This is the most frequently available member of the genus. Hatchetfishes spend almost all their time just below the water's surface, waiting for insects to fall into the water. Their natural reaction to anything that scares them is to jump, and they are powerful leapers. Any aquarium housing them must be completely covered. The other members of the genus are also good choices for nano-tanks, and their behavior and requirements are the same. Avoid the larger hatchetfishes from other genera for nano-tanks.

NATIVE RANGE: Widespread in the Amazon River basin

MAXIMUM SIZE: 1.5 in. (4 cm)

MINIMUM AQUARIUM SIZE: 10 gal. (38 L)

WATER PARAMETERS: pH 6–7.5, soft to moderate, 74–80°F (23–27°C)

FEEDING: Carnivore. Feed floating dry foods and be sure to include live foods, such as wingless fruit flies, in the diet.

BEHAVIOR & CARE: Hatchetfishes are shy, schooling fishes that are easily intimidated by fast-moving or larger tankmates. They do best when housed with fishes their own size or smaller or with relatively slow-moving larger species. A very appealing community can be created by adding a school of Cardinal Tetras, a school of either *Trigonostigma espei* or *T. hengeli*, and a school of Marbled Hatchets. This is particularly effective in tanks at least 16 inches (41 cm) tall, where the fish population will separate into natural layers. The colors and shapes of these species work very well together aesthetically, especially in a well-planted aquarium with a dark substrate.

SILVERTIP TETRA *Hasemania nana*
(Copper Tetra)

OVERVIEW: These are readily available and an excellent schooling fish for the beginner aquarist with a community aquarium. Like most tetras, they do well in a peaceful community, and proof that they are thriving is when you spy small, silver slivers hovering over the substrate detritus. They will spawn in a community setting and, provided there is a good diet for all and plenty of cover, some fry will survive to keep the population steady.

NATIVE RANGE: Brazil, Rio Sao Francisco basin
MAXIMUM LENGTH: 2 in. (5 cm)
MINIMUM AQUARIUM SIZE: 20 gal. (70 L)
WATER: pH 6.0–8.0, hardness 5–20°dGH, 74–82°F (23–28°C)
FEEDING: Omnivore. Accepts small prepared aquarium foods supplemented with small live or frozen foods, such as brine shrimp, *Daphnia*, and *Cyclops*.
BEHAVIOR & CARE: The Silvertip is comfortable with fine substrate and some driftwood and fine-leaved plants, especially Java Moss. Add dried oak leaves to simulate "leaf litter" and to acidify the water. The male is the slimmer and more colorful fish. Females get fat when gravid. Soft, acidic water, dim lights, and protection for the adhesive eggs will generally result in at least some fry escaping predation. Ideal tankmates include other small tetras, most livebearers, danios, *Corydoras*, and most of the available gouramis and dwarf cichlids.

GLOWLIGHT TETRA *Hemigrammus erythrozonus*

OVERVIEW: This fish is native to quiet jungle streams with tannin-stained water and lazy water currents. This is a very popular community fish because a school provides great color and action without nippiness. Most aquarium stock is mass produced, so it is an excellent beginner's fish. It is also available in an albino form. A large shoal of a dozen or more makes for a very pleasing and natural display.

NATIVE RANGE: Guyana, Essequibo River

MAXIMUM LENGTH: 1.5 in (4 cm)

MINIMUM AQUARIUM SIZE: 20 gal. (70 L)

WATER: pH 5.5–7.5, hardness 0–12°dGH, 75–82°F (24–28°C)

FEEDING: Omnivore. Accepts small prepared aquarium foods supplemented with small live or frozen foods. Offer pigment-enhancing dried specialty foods and *Cyclops* (frozen or dry CYCLOP-EEZE®) to help maintain their bright coloration.

BEHAVIOR & CARE: Six or more Glowlights will illuminate a dappled blackwater biotope. Use blackwater extract, a sandy substrate, and driftwood for an authentic feel. It can be combined with other *Hemigrammus* or *Hyphessobrycon* species, pencilfishes, or *Apistogrammas* for a biotope tank, or with the majority of commonly available species of danios, rasboras, tetras, livebearers, *Corydoras*, or smaller Loricariids. As with most fishes of its stature, it should not be housed with larger species that could see it as food, like angelfishes. A similar species is *Hemigrammus pulcher*, the Pretty Tetra.

RUMMYNOSE TETRA *Hemigrammus rhodostomus*
(True Rummynose Tetra)

OVERVIEW: These tetras are famous for their use as a companion to Discus (*Symphysodon* spp.) They are especially effective in a group of a dozen fishes, as they are tight schoolers—unlike some other shoaling fishes that seem to barely know one another. The snout is pale first thing in the morning, but soon brightens up. If the red snout looks washed out at other times, check the water quality immediately. They are like canaries in a coal mine as far as water quality is concerned. Very similar to *Hemigrammus bleheri*, which is also sold as the Rummynose Tetra. A third Rummynose look-alike is *Petitella georgiae*. Despite being different species from two different genera, all three have the same requirements and exhibit the same behaviors.

NATIVE RANGE: Blackwater rivers in the Amazon River basin

MAXIMUM SIZE: 2 in. (5 cm)

MINIMUM AQUARIUM SIZE: 10 gal. (38 L)

WATER PARAMETERS: 5.5–7.5, soft to moderate preferred but will adapt to harder, more alkaline, 74–84°F (23–29°C)

FEEDING: Omnivore. Feed small, dry foods supplemented with frozen and live foods. *Cyclops*, baby brine shrimp, and color-enhancing rations will help intensify the red pigmentation.

BEHAVIOR & CARE: An active, schooling species that generally inhabits the lower half of the aquarium. The bigger the school, the happier they are. They show their best colors in well-planted tanks with dark substrates. Mix well with similarly sized hatchetfishes, rasboras, danionins, catfishes, labyrinth fishes, and peaceful cichlids.

FIREHEAD RUMMYNOSE TETRA *Hemigrammus bleheri*
(Rummynose Tetra, Firehead Tetra)
NATIVE RANGE: Rio Negro, Rio Meta Rivers, Brazil, Colombia
MAXIMUM SIZE: 2 in. (5 cm)
MINIMUM AQUARIUM SIZE: 10 gal. (38 L)

FALSE RUMMYNOSE TETRA *Petitella georgiae*
(Rummynose Tetra)
NATIVE RANGE: Rio Purus, Rio Negro, Rio Madeira, Peru, Brazil
MAXIMUM SIZE: 2 in. (5 cm)
MINIMUM AQUARIUM SIZE: 10 gal. (38 L)

GOLD TETRA *Hemigrammus rodwayi*
(Golden Tetra)

OVERVIEW: Despite the common name, the gold color is seen only in wild fish and is a reaction to the infestation of a trematode parasite that causes a concentration of guanine in the skin. Captive-bred fish are silver, so wild fish are definitely preferred. Gold-colored fish were originally described as a different species, *H. armstrongi*, and are still frequently referred to by that name, though it is a junior synonym of *H. rodwayi.* Most imports of this wide-ranging species come from Colombia.

NATIVE RANGE: Peru, Colombia, Venezuela, Guyana, Suriname, French Guiana, Brazil

MAXIMUM SIZE: 1.75 in. (4.5 cm)

MINIMUM AQUARIUM SIZE: 5 gal. (19 L)

WATER PARAMETERS: Not critical, 74–80°F (23–27°C)

FEEDING: Omnivore. Offer fine, dry food and small frozen and live meaty foods, including enriched brine shrimp, *Daphnia*, *Mysis*, *Cyclops*, and pigment-enhancing rations.

BEHAVIOR & CARE: Looks best when kept in a school of at least 8–10 fish in a brightly lit, well-planted aquarium. A planted aquarium housing only a large school of gold tetras can be very impressive. This species generally schools higher in the water column than *Paracheirodon* or *Hyphessobrycon* species, so it looks good with them. Also suitable as tankmates for small catfishes, labyrinth fishes, and peaceful dwarf cichlids.

EMBER TETRA *Hyphessobrycon amandae*

OVERVIEW: A truly nano-scale tetra, this attractive little species is no longer as rare as it once was. With their bright copper coloring and peaceful nature, they are an excellent choice for a small planted tank featuring driftwood and plants. This species lives in quiet, acidic blackwaters.

NATIVE RANGE: Rio Araguaia basin, Brazil

MAXIMUM SIZE: 0.8 in. (2 cm)

MINIMUM AQUARIUM SIZE: 5 gal. (19 L)

WATER PARAMETERS: pH 5.5–7.5, 75–82°F (24–28°C)

FEEDING: Omnivore. Readily accepts quality flake and does well when offered a varied diet of small live and frozen foods such as *Cyclops*, baby brine shrimp, *Daphnia*, and Golden Pearls, a micro-pelleted ration.

BEHAVIOR & CARE: Ember Tetras, like all schooling species, do best in groups of eight or more. They can be shy, so having a larger number increases their confidence. Appropriate tankmates include *Aspidoras*, dwarf *Corydoras*, pencilfishes, and *Otocinclus*. Boisterous tankmates should be avoided, as well as those who could easily eat them, like angels and some gouramis. They can be housed with dwarf shrimp, though dense areas of plants like moss are required to limit predation upon young shrimp. Use a mesh bag of peat moss in the filter to mimic its natural water conditions, or add a blackwater extract. When not kept in acidic conditions, it may lose the intensity of its colors.

SERPAE TETRA *Hyphessobrycon eques*
(Fire Tetra, Red Tetra)

OVERVIEW: This is a glorious fish for a large, planted nano-aquarium, boasting brilliant and even glittering colors with jet-black highlights and a bold attitude that brings it out front and center. It is also a fish with a reputation for scrappiness and fin-nipping. Its worst characteristics are revealed if it is crowded or placed in a community with timid species. Having a shoal of at least six or more will help dispel the aggression; 10 or more is even better. A similar-looking fish, the Red Phantom Tetra, *H. sweglesi*, is less aggressive.

NATIVE RANGE: Rio Guapore, Rio Paraguay, Argentina, Paraguay, Brazil

MAXIMUM LENGTH: 1.6 in. (4 cm)

MINIMUM AQUARIUM SIZE: 15 gal. (57 L)

WATER: pH 5.5–7.5, hardness 0–12°dGH, 72–82°F (22–28°C)

FEEDING: Omnivore. Should be offered a variety of dried quality flake as well as frozen bloodworms, *Daphnia*, *Cyclops*, enriched adult brine shrimp, mysid shrimp, and high quality pellets and flakes. Condition for breeding with live brine shrimp, *Daphnia*, etc.

BEHAVIOR & CARE: A well-planted tank with a dark substrate and treatment with peat is the best way to see the spectacular colors of this fish. The male is distinguished by his almost fully black dorsal fin. Females have a heavier stature. Use a mature aquarium with protection for the eggs if spawning is the goal, as the parents will eat them as soon as they are laid.

LEMON TETRA *Hyphessobrycon pulchripinnis*

OVERVIEW: One of the loveliest and most peaceful tetras for a planted or small community aquarium, the Lemon Tetra is ideal for an Amazon biotope tank. It is widely available and a great fish for the beginner, while more advanced aquarists who keep it in shoals of 10 or more use it to great effect in planted aquariums.

NATIVE RANGE: Rio Tapajos basin, Brazil

MAXIMUM SIZE: 1.6 in. (4 cm)

MINIMUM AQUARIUM SIZE: 15 gal. (57 L)

WATER PARAMETERS: pH 5.5-7.5, 75-82°F (24-28°C)

FEEDING: Omnivore. Should be offered a variety of dried quality flake as well as frozen bloodworms, *Daphnia*, *Cyclops*, enriched adult brine shrimp, mysid shrimp, and high quality pellets and flakes.

BEHAVIOR & CARE: Hardy and inexpensive, this fish is easily bred in a species tank utilizing spawning mops or Java Moss. They can be spawned in a group, and they should always be kept in group-ings of six or more. In a community aquarium, they can be kept with most comparable-sized fishes, including tetras, catfishes, loaches, gouramis, and dwarf cichlids. A similiar species is the so-called Pretty Tetra, *Hemigrammus pulcher*. For an Amazon biotope, use a river-sand bottom, pieces of driftwood and gnarled roots or tree branches, dried leaves, and plantings of different species of Amazon swords, *Echinodorus* spp.

RED PHANTOM TETRA *Hyphessobrycon sweglesi*
(*Megalamphodus sweglesi*)

OVERVIEW: Like its cousin *H. megalopterus*, the Black Phantom Tetra, this tetra is better known in its old genus, *Megalamphodus*, and is a schooling species, preferring to be in groups of 10 or more. It is best maintained in a heavily planted tank; otherwise, its colors become noticeably muted. A related and very appealing nano fish of the same size is the Flame Tetra, *H. flammeus*, from eastern Brazil.

NATIVE RANGE: Upper Orinoco drainage, Colombia

MAXIMUM LENGTH: 1.5 in. (4 cm)

MINIMUM AQUARIUM SIZE: 15 gal. (57 L)

WATER: pH 5.5–7.5, hardness 0–12°dGH, 68–73°F (20–23°C)

FEEDING: Omnivore. Easy to feed, it will accept most dried foods but should be offered a variety small live, frozen, and prepared foods including high protein worms and enriched brine shrimp.

BEHAVIOR & CARE: This fish should not be kept too warm (including for breeding), and prefers soft, acid water and subdued lighting. Floating plants and dark substrate will encourage its best colors. An ideal community would include dwarf cichlids and catfish species with similar water requirements. The female has a red, white, and black dorsal fin; the male's is larger and red. Condition to breed with live foods. Use a breeding tank with very soft water at pH 5.5–6.0, fine-leaved plants, spawning mesh, and dim light. Often delicate upon import, it is sensitive to poor water quality and needs a decent regime of tank maintenance.

DIPTAIL PENCILFISH *Nannostomus eques*
(Tube Mouth Pencilfish, Rocket Pencilfish, Hockey Stick Pencilfish, Auratus Pencilfish)

OVERVIEW: This is a unique species that swims at an angle with its head up. Three distinct color forms exist in the wild. In the "standard" form the caudal fin has a black lower lobe, and in the red-tailed form from the regions of Puerto Inirida and Puerto Gaitan in Colombia the lower lobe of the caudal fin is red. Specimens originating in eastern Brazil and exported from Belem have black caudal lobes and blue horizontal stripes on the body. It is likely that these three forms will eventually be considered separate species. Due to its tiny mouth and shy nature, care must be taken in a mixed community to ensure that this species gets its share of food or it will slowly starve to death. Males are more slender than females.

NATIVE RANGE: Northern South America from Peru through Venezuela, Colombia, Guyana, Brazil

MAXIMUM SIZE: 2 in. (5 cm)

MINIMUM AQUARIUM SIZE: 5 gal. (19 L)

WATER PARAMETERS: pH 5-7.5, soft, 72-80°F (22-27°C)

FEEDING: Carnivore. Tiny live food is the best diet. Will accept suitably sized dry and frozen foods such as *Cyclops* and *Daphnia*.

BEHAVIOR & CARE: Best suited for a well planted, moderately lit aquarium with a low flow rate. Must be kept in a school and the larger the group, the better. Easily intimidated by faster swimmers. Ideal tankmate for licorice gouramis and other slow, shy species.

CORAL RED PENCILFISH *Nannostomus mortenthaleri*
(Mortenthaler's Pencilfish, Peru Red Pencilfish)

OVERVIEW: When it was introduced recently, the Coral Red Pencilfish became an immediate hit within the aquarium hobby. With its gentle disposition and striking colors, it stands out in a well-planted community or species aquarium.

NATIVE RANGE: Nanay and Rio Tigre River basins, Peru

MAXIMUM LENGTH: 1.5 in. (4 cm)

MINIMUM AQUARIUM SIZE: 10 gal. (35 L)

WATER: pH 6.5–7.0, hardness 0–10°dGH, 75–78°F (24–26°C)

FEEDING: Micropredator. Easy to supplement with good quality flake foods, they show the best color and condition when fed a varied diet including frozen foods like *Cyclops*, *Daphnia*, or baby brine shrimp.

BEHAVIOR & CARE: Ideally kept in groups of more females than males in a heavily planted tank with a dark substrate. The addition of floating plants, Java Moss, and leaf litter are invaluable for encouraging spawning and preserving fry with this consummate egg-eater. Gentle filtration and a well-established aquarium are required for this peaceful species. Adult males are noticeably stockier and more colorful than females. The males also have a white marking at the anterior base of the dorsal fin. They are an expensive, but desirable fish best maintained on its own for breeding, or with other small characids or loraticariids. It is also an ideal dither fish for *Apistogramma* species. Fry can be reared using infusoria or white worms.

DWARF PENCILFISH *Nannostomus marginatus*

OVERVIEW: A classic nano fish, this is a tiny and peaceful species, although not quite the smallest in its genus. It has a wide range in South America east of the Andes and exists in different geographical color forms. It is a very timid fish and is best kept in groups of five to 10 or more to encourage bolder behaviors. Appropriate tankmates include dwarf cichlids, small characins, and small catfishes. Avoid large or excessively outgoing species and provide ample plantings and floating vegetation to offer a sense of security.

NATIVE RANGE: Brazil, Guyana, Suriname, Colombia, Peru

MAXIMUM SIZE: 1.4 in. (3.5 cm)

MINIMUM AQUARIUM SIZE: 10 gal. (38 L)

WATER: pH 6.5–7.0, hardness 0–10°dGH, 75–78°F (24–26°C)

FEEDING: Micropredator. A varied diet consisting of live worms and frozen foods like *Cyclops*, *Daphnia*, or baby brine shrimp is best. They will also readily take dried foods, like flake.

BEHAVIOR & CARE: Males form a dominance heirarchy in mixed shoals It is important to have a good ratio of sexes and to provide ample areas of dense planting to break up lines of sight and provide space for multiple territories. Leaf litter, and the tannins and microorganisms it produces, are invaluable when attempting to breed this fish. Mop spawning is a good strategy, and the parents or the mop can be removed after two or three days of the first spawning behavior.

NEON TETRA *Paracheirodon innesi*

OVERVIEW: The evolutionary explanation for the classic neon stripe in these related species suggests that, in its natural blackwater habitat, the stripe is less visible when viewed from the side than from above, where it may aid in predator evasion by projecting mirror images onto the surface of the water. This fools the predator into thinking the tetra is where it is not. Regardless of why the stripe is there, aquarists the world over appreciate its presence. It sets these three species apart and gives them their popularity, which is enhanced by their peaceful, schooling nature.

NATIVE RANGE: Blackwater Tributaries of the Amazon River

MAXIMUM SIZE: 1.2 in. (3 cm)

MINIMUM AQUARIUM SIZE: 10 gal. (38 L)

WATER PARAMETERS: pH 5.5–8, soft to moderate, 70–82°F (21–28°C), with neons at the low end of the range, green neons in the middle, and cardinals on the upper end.

FEEDING: Carnivore. Feed high quality dry foods and supplement with frozen and live foods.

BEHAVIOR & CARE: Very peaceful. At their best in well planted, well lit aquariums with non-threatening tankmates. Excellent choices include pencilfishes, other small tetras, small rasboras, small Corydoradinae and loricariid catfish, small-mouthed labyrinth fishes, and small shrimp. Cardinal Tetras are still imported in large numbers from the wild and choosing wild fish supports a sustainable fishery, which in turn encourages the indigenous peoples to protect its environment.

CARDINAL TETRA *Paracheirodon axelrodi*
NATIVE RANGE: Rio Negro, Brazil, and Orinoco watershed, Venezuela
MAXIMUM SIZE: 1.75 in. (4 cm)
MINIMUM AQUARIUM SIZE: 10 gal. (38 L)

GREEN NEON TETRA *Paracheirodon simulans*
NATIVE RANGE: Rio Negro, Brazil, and Orinoco watershed, Venezuela
MAXIMUM SIZE: 1.25 in. (3 cm)
MINIMUM AQUARIUM SIZE: 10 gal. (38 L)

CHARACIN – TETRA • PEACEFUL

BLOTCHED PYRRHULINA *Pyrrhulina spilota*

OVERVIEW: The ideal dither fish for most *Apistogramma* or *Pelvicachromis* dwarf cichlids, these delightful and eyecatching characins are still uncommon to find in the trade but perfectly suited to this task. With their subtle coloring, interesting breeding behavior, and outgoing personality, they make an excellent upper-water-layer species for any dwarf cichlid breeding tank.

NATIVE RANGE: Upper Amazon River basin, Peru

MAXIMUM SIZE: 2.7 in. (7 cm)

MINIMUM AQUARIUM SIZE: 20 gal. (76 L)

WATER PARAMETERS: pH 5-7, 75–80°F (24–27°C)

FEEDING: Micropredator. Does best on an initial diet of live *Cyclops* or *Daphnia* but is easily transitioned after acclimation to comparable frozen, meaty foods.

BEHAVIOR & CARE: These fish stay very near the surface and are prone to jumping, so lots of surface vegetation or a tight-fitting lid is required. They are peaceful, ignoring the fry of other fishes. The females lay their eggs on submerged plant leaves and the males guard first the eggs, then the brood. They are difficult to obtain, but a perfect addition to a community dwarf cichlid tank. They would also do well with most peaceful community fishes like tetras or *Corydoras,* though one should avoid placing them in a tank with other top-water-dwelling species. When added to provide "dithering" services, their activity and confident presence in the water column tend to make shy species feel secure and act with greater boldness.

AGASSIZ'S DWARF CICHLID *Apistogramma agassizii*

OVERVIEW: This is a classic dwarf cichlid and a highly variable species with many geographic morphs and captive-bred color forms. Several geographic morphs have been raised to species status and more splitting is likely to occur. Spawns readily, so fish from different locations or with different color patterns should not be kept together if the hobbyist doesn't want to risk unintended hybridization. Males are larger and more colorful, with a spade-shaped caudal fin. Bright yellow color on the female indicates impending or existing spawn.

NATIVE RANGE: Amazon River basin

MAXIMUM SIZE: Males 3 in. (8 cm), females 2 in. (5 cm)

MINIMUM AQUARIUM SIZE: 15 gal. (57 L)

WATER PARAMETERS: pH 5-6.8, soft preferred but adapts to harder, 72-84°F (22-29°C)

FEEDING: Feed high quality flakes and pellets along with frozen foods. Supplemental feeding of live foods, such as mosquito larvae, *Daphnia*, *Cyclops*, and Grindal worms, is beneficial, particularly if spawning is desired.

BEHAVIOR & CARE: This is an active and outgoing species. A female defends a small territory around a spawning site (small ceramic caves built for this purpose are readily available), while the male maintains a larger territory. Best maintained as a pair in a species tank or with tankmates large and robust enough to be on the receiving end of some aggression. Excellent tankmates include *Hyphessobrycon* species, danios, and small *Melanotaenia*.

UMBRELLA DWARF CICHLID *Apistogramma borellii*
(Borelli's Dwarf Cichlid)

OVERVIEW: This is another variable small cichlid species with different captive-bred forms and several geographic morphs. It is commonly bred in Asia, and shipments from there tend to be made up of mostly males. More peaceful than the other Apistos included here, so a better choice for a community. Bright yellow color on the female indicates impending or existing spawn.

NATIVE RANGE: Paraguay River basin into Argentina

MAXIMUM SIZE: Males 2.5 in. (6.4 cm), females 1.75 in. (4.5 cm)

MINIMUM AQUARIUM SIZE: 15 gal. (57 L)

WATER PARAMETERS: pH 6–7.5, soft preferred but adapts to harder, 76–80°F (24–27°C)

FEEDING: Offer a variety of foods, including high quality flakes and pellets along with frozen foods. Supplemental feeding of live foods such as mosquito larvae, *Daphnia*, *Cyclops*, and Grindal worms is beneficial, particularly if spawning is desired.

BEHAVIOR & CARE: *A. borellii* is initially somewhat shy. Aquarium décor should include driftwood and plants with numerous caves (small ceramic caves built for this purpose are readily available). During reproduction, the female defends a small territory around a spawning site while the male maintains a larger territory. Peaceful schooling tankmates, such as small tetras, nano-sized rainbow-fishes, or rasboras will help it to overcome its shyness. Becomes bolder over time.

COCKATOO CICHLID *Apistogramma cacatuoides*

OVERVIEW: In its courtship colors, this is a flamboyantly pigmented dwarf cichlid and probably the easiest Apisto for beginners to spawn. In addition to a number of naturally occurring color morphs, selectively bred forms exist in a variety of colors and patterns. It is likely that some of the wild forms will be raised to species status, so unintended hybridization is possible in the aquarium. Males sport extended spiny dorsal rays and extended caudal fins and are much more colorful than females. A dramatic female color change, usually to yellow, indicates readiness to spawn or that a spawn has occurred. The female cares for the eggs and fry.

NATIVE RANGE: Upper Amazon River drainage

MAXIMUM SIZE: Males 2.5 in. (6.4 cm), females 1.75 in. (4.5 cm)

MINIMUM AQUARIUM SIZE: 15 gal. (57 L)

WATER PARAMETERS: pH 6.0–7.5, hardness unimportant, 76–80°F (24–27°C)

FEEDING: Feed high quality flakes and pellets, plus frozen foods and occasional live foods, such as mosquito larvae, *Daphnia*, *Cyclops*, and Grindal worms.

BEHAVIOR & CARE: This is a territorial species best maintained in pairs. The male's territory will include the smaller territory of the female. Can be rough on tankmates when spawning, so other fishes should be robust. Décor should consist of driftwood and live plants and include several caves of wood, rocks, flowerpots, coconut shells, or ceramic. A single male is a better community resident than a pair in a small tank.

CHECKERBOARD CICHLID *Dicrossus filamentosus*
(Lyretail Checkerboard Cichlid)

OVERVIEW: The body colors and lyretail of the males make for a very impressive package. Another species, *D. maculatus*, features a body pattern that is more truly a checkerboard, but its finnage is no match for that of *D. filamentosus*. This species is usually available as young, wild-caught fish from the Rio Negro or Rio Inirida. Sexing the young fish is difficult, so be careful to pick out fish that seem to be doing very well, are alert, and are feeding and breathing normally.

NATIVE RANGE: Blackwater habitats of the Rio Negro, Rio Orinoco, and Rio Inirida

MAXIMUM SIZE: 2.5 in. (6.4 cm)

MINIMUM AQUARIUM SIZE: 15 gal. (57 L)

WATER PARAMETERS: 5–7.5, soft to moderately hard, 76–84°F (24–29°C)

FEEDING: Omnivore. Checkerboards will accept dry foods including those for carnivores and those for herbivores, but their long-term health requires a more varied diet that includes frozen and live foods. *Daphnia*, *Cyclops*, mosquito larvae, and brine shrimp are all excellent selections.

BEHAVIOR & CARE: Checkerboard Cichlids can be a little tough to get established in the home aquarium, but once they settle in they do very well. They will get over their initial shyness as long as tankmates don't bully them. Checkerboards should be the only cichlids in the tank. Suitable tankmates include smaller tetras, rasboras, loaches, and catfishes.

MASKED JULIDOCHROMIS *Julidochromis transcriptus*
(Masked Julie)

OVERVIEW: Here is an interesting African cichlid that can be housed in a nano-aquarium. Care and maintenance is the same for all the morphs. It is a relatively peaceful species when not spawning. The slightly larger *J. ornatus* and *J. dickfeldi* are similar in all respects and can be kept in a 20-gallon aquarium. There are several geographic morphs, the most popular of which is *J. transcriptus* "Gombi."

NATIVE RANGE: Lake Tanganyika

MAXIMUM SIZE: 2.75 in. (7 cm)

MINIMUM AQUARIUM SIZE: 20 gal. (76 L)

WATER PARAMETERS: Hard and alkaline, 74–82°F (23–28°C)

FEEDING: Omnivore. Feeds primarily on benthic crustaceans and other prey but also ingests aufwuchs (algal turfs with microfauna) while feeding. Offer a diet high in protein and include frozen and live foods while also occasionally feeding *Spirulina*-based flakes or pellets.

BEHAVIOR & CARE: Stack a pile of rocks along the back and/or sides of the aquarium to provide caves for this rock-dwelling species. Will spawn in caves in a community tank. They make excellent parents whose brood care can include eliminating all tankmates, although offspring from successive clutches may be allowed to remain in the parent's territory. Single specimens are great in a tank set up for *Neolamprologus multifasciatus*. Other suitable tankmates include active species that will do well in similar water conditions, such as certain danios and small *Melanotaenia* rainbowfishes.

FLAG CICHLID *Laetacara curviceps*
(Flag Acara, Dwarf Flag Cichlid)

OVERVIEW: This is a chunky-bodied, extremely peaceful fish that might be the ideal nano-tank cichlid. Males and females are similarly colored, making them very difficult to sex. In mature adults, the male's dorsal and anal fins are slightly longer, and ripe females are broader-bodied than males. The black spot on the dorsal may be larger in females. Several geographic morphs exist in the wild but almost all fish available to hobbyists are commercially bred.

NATIVE RANGE: Lower portion of the Amazon River basin, Brazil

MAXIMUM SIZE: 3 in. (8 cm)

MINIMUM AQUARIUM SIZE: 15 gal. (57 L)

WATER PARAMETERS: pH 6–7.5, moderate hardness, 74–82°F (23–28°C)

FEEDING: Omnivore. Diet should include high quality flakes and pellets, both those designed for carnivores and *Spirulina*-based for herbivores, along with frozen and live foods. Frozen peas with the outer skins removed are a real treat.

BEHAVIOR & CARE: Prefers dimly lit aquariums with some driftwood overhangs and plants in which to hide. Peaceful schooling species such as pencilfishes, hatchetfishes, and Corydoradinae catfishes are good choices as tankmates. Flag cichlids will almost never bother other species unless they are defending eggs or fry. This is an open spawner that forms permanent pair bonds and prefers to spawn on a flat rock. After hatching the fry will be moved to pits dug in the substrate.

OCELLATED SHELL-DWELLER *Lamprologus ocellatus*
(Ocellated Lamp)

OVERVIEW: A dwarf African charmer, this is one of the most loved of the shell-dwelling "Lamps" from Lake Tanganyika. These fish live on the sand beds along the edge of the lake in areas that are littered with the empty shells of dead *Neothauma* snails. The cichlids live and breed in the shells in a fascinating adaptation to the only shelter available in this habitat. This species is available in several color forms, and males are somewhat larger and more colorful than females.

NATIVE RANGE: Lake Tanganyika

MAXIMUM SIZE: 2.5 in. (6.4 cm)

MINIMUM AQUARIUM SIZE: 10 gal. (38 L)

WATER PARAMETERS: pH 7–8.5, hard, 76–82°F (24–28°C)

FEEDING: Predator. Feed a variety of prepared foods appropriate to the size of the fish and regularly mix up the diet by adding frozen foods such as *Mysis* shrimp and enriched adult brine shrimp. Supplement with occasional feedings of live foods.

BEHAVIOR & CARE: Females maintain small territories within the confines of the male's territory. These are very entertaining fish to watch. They can be mixed with the smaller *Julidochromis* species in 20-gallon (76-L) tanks. Other tankmates should be able to live in similar water conditions. Small *Melanotaenia* species and the traditional danionins are good choices. Catfishes also work well.

CICHLID • TERRITORIAL

93

RAM *Mikrogeophagus ramirezi*
(Butterfly Cichlid)

OVERVIEW: This is one of the smallest geophagine (earth-eating) cichlids and a true classic among dwarf cichlid enthusiasts. There are a number of captive-bred color variants, including the "Electric German Blue" shown above, and long-finned varieties. If you want to have a pair, the best way is to observe the fish for a while prior to purchase. It is common even in a dealer's tank to observe the formation of pair bonds, and it's relatively straightforward to purchase those two fish.

NATIVE RANGE: Orinoco River basin, Colombia and Venezuela

MAXIMUM SIZE: 2 in. (5 cm)

MINIMUM AQUARIUM SIZE: 10 gal. (38 L)

WATER PARAMETERS: pH 5.5–7.5, soft to moderate, 76–84°F (24–29°C)

FEEDING: Omnivore. In nature, it sifts mouthfuls of the substrate for edible bits.

Rams feed readily on most foods, including dry and frozen foods. Gel-based foods can be particularly useful, especially for wild fish, as it allows them to replicate their natural feeding behavior.

BEHAVIOR & CARE: Rams may be shy initially but they rapidly overcome this as they adjust to their surroundings. They should be the focal point of the fish community, and care should be taken to provide tankmates that will not intimidate them. This species is a substrate spawner that will spawn in the community tank, although it is not likely to successfully raise its fry in that environment. Must be quarantined at first and treated for gill flukes.

BANDED SHELL-DWELLER *Neolamprologus multifasciatus*
(Multistripe Shell-Dweller)

OVERVIEW: This is the smallest known cichlid. It lives in the sand zone, where it inhabits empty snail shells. Each fish has its own shell. Males maintain territories, within which females maintain smaller territories centered on their own shells. The male visits the female's shell to fertilize her eggs. Capable of moving shells to a desired location. While these fish can be kept without shells, their natural behavior will be disrupted and they won't be as interesting.

NATIVE RANGE: Lake Tanganyika

MAXIMUM SIZE: 1.75 in. (4.5 cm)

MINIMUM AQUARIUM SIZE: 10 gal. (38 L)

WATER PARAMETERS: Hard and alkaline, 76–82°F (24–28°C)

FEEDING: Carnivore. Offer a varied diet high in protein and including a range of frozen foods. Occasional feedings of live foods such as baby brine shrimp, *Daphnia*, and *Cyclops* are also beneficial.

BEHAVIOR & CARE: While plants and rocks can be added around the edges, most of the substrate should consist of fine sand with more empty snail shells than the number of fish. Mystery Snail shells work well, as do any number of small univalve shells available through the shell trade. Shells of unknown origin should be boiled prior to using, though boiling may discolor them. This species is highly prolific and the population will increase. Tankmates should be active in the upper water column. Danios, like *Danio rerio,* the zebra danio, and similar species, and small *Melanotaenia* species make particularly good choices.

CICHLID • TERRITORIAL

COMMON KRIBENSIS *Pelvicachromis pulcher*
(Krib, Kribensis, Rainbow Krib)

OVERVIEW: Affectionately known as the "Krib," this is one of the most commonly kept and popular species of dwarf cichlid. They are widely available as captive-bred specimens and are adaptable to a range of water parameters. Different color variations are available from captive-bred sources.

NATIVE RANGE: West Africa, Cameroon, Nigeria

MAXIMUM SIZE: Males 4 in. (10 cm), females 3 in. (7.5 cm)

MINIMUM AQUARIUM SIZE: 20 gal. (76 L) for a pair

WATER PARAMETERS: pH 5–7.5, 75–80°F (24–27°C)

FEEDING: Omnivore. *Pelvicachromis* are easy to feed, readily accepting pelleted or frozen foods. To condition to breed, a mix of frozen or live worms and invertebrates is ideal. Colonies can be maintained with small pellets or high quality flake.

BEHAVIOR & CARE: *Pelvicachromis* are predominantly found in slow-moving streams and rivers with dense vegetation. Add coconut caves, stacked driftwood, and areas of dense planting of species like *Anubias* or Java Fern to ensure they have ample breeding spots. They exhibit strong parental care and actively guide their young around the tank for about six weeks. At this point it is a good idea to separate the young, as the adult pair will predate on the fry in order to spawn again. The parents will actively chase other fishes, so tankmates should be sturdy and of a decent size. *Pyrrhulina* cf. *spilota* are a good choice. This fish is one of the best choices for beginners trying cichlids and breeding; it is a manageable size, easy to feed, and exhibits interesting spawning behaviors.

STRIPED KRIBENSIS *Pelvicachromis taeniatus*

OVERVIEW: This sister species to the Common Kribensis is a sexually dimorphic, cave-spawning dwarf cichlid. There are numerous unique geographic races in the trade; common forms include "Moliwe," "Wouri," "Nigeria Red," and "Bipindi." There are also many others. Generally speaking, the females get a rich red/purple belly, and the males have a checkerboard pattern at the top of the caudal fin. Strikingly beautiful when in spawning dress, they are an excellent breeding project for the devoted hobbyist.

NATIVE RANGE: West Africa, Cameroon, Nigeria

MAXIMUM SIZE: 4 in. (10 cm)

MINIMUM AQUARIUM SIZE: 20 gal. (76 L) for a pair

WATER PARAMETERS: pH 5–7.5, 70–75°F (21–24°C)

FEEDING: Omnivore. Offer a variety of dry, frozen, and live foods. To condition to breed, a mix of frozen or live worms and invertebrates is ideal.

BEHAVIOR & CARE: This species usually lives in quiet streams and rivers with lots of plant growth. They practice strong parental care and shepherd their young around the aquarium for about six weeks. After that we advise separating the young; the adult pair will predate on the fry in preparation for further spawning. Choose hardy, good-sized tankmates that can withstand being chased by the parents. Avoid keeping small or delicate fishes, as the parents will actively defend their breeding territory and protect their fry. Species tanks will yield the highest numbers of fry. Adding coconut-shell caves, stacked driftwood, and densely planted species like *Anubias* or Java Fern gives them plenty of breeding site choices.

CHILI RASBORA *Boraras brigittae*
(Mosquito Rasbora, Blood Rasbora)

OVERVIEW: The dimunitive Chili Rasbora is currently one of the most popular nano-fish species because of its striking red coloration and its versatility for a small tank. This, and other similar *Boraras* species, are so tiny that they are commonly referred to as "eyestrain rasboras," but despite their small size they make a big impact and are hardy, even suitable for the beginner aquarist. Keep in groups of 8 to 10 (or more).

NATIVE RANGE: Endemic to Southwestern Borneo

MAXIMUM SIZE: 0.8 in. (2 cm)

MINIMUM AQUARIUM SIZE: 2.5 gal. (10 L)

WATER PARAMETERS: pH 5–7, 73–82°F (23–28°C)

FEEDING: Micropredator. It readily accepts small dried or frozen foods such as *Cyclops*, Golden Pearls, frozen baby *Artemia*, or *Daphnia*, along with good quality color-enhancing flake foods.

BEHAVIOR & CARE: *Boraras* spp. are very peaceful fishes, but can be a bit timid and do best when housed with other species of a similar temperament (*Sundadanio*, *Triginostigma*, *Brevibora*, other *Boraras*, small *Corydoras*, *Aspidoras*, *Otocinclus* catfishes). It is also a good choice to pair with small anabantoids, like *Parosphromenus* or the smallest of the wild betta types. Avoid pairing them with fishes that are much larger or have a very boisterious nature. *Boraras* spp. appreciate a densely planted tank with a sandy substrate and some driftwood or leaf litter. Tannins intensify their colors, and the decomposing leaf litter and wood help provide microorganisms that are a helpful secondary food.

LEAST RASBORA *Boraras micros*
(Least Boraras)
NATIVE RANGE: Mekong River basin, Laos and northern Thailand
MAXIMUM SIZE: 0.5 inch (1.3 cm)
MINIMUM AQUARIUM SIZE: 2.5 gal. (10 L)

EXCLAMATION POINT RASBORA *Boraras uropthalmoides*
(Least Rasbora, Exclamation Point Boraras)
NATIVE RANGE: Mekong River basin, Thailand, Laos, Cambodia, Vietnam, Island of Sumatra
MAXIMUM SIZE: 0.6 inch (1.6 cm)
MINIMUM AQUARIUM SIZE: 2.5 gal. (10 L)

EMERALD-EYE RASBORA *Brevibora dorsiocellata*
(Greeneye Rasbora, Eyespot Rasbora, Hi-Spot Rasbora)

OVERVIEW: Noteworthy for its exceptionally tight schooling habit, the Emerald-Eye Rasbora stays in the top third of the tank. With their bright lamp eye and subtle coloration, they make a striking impact in a heavily planted tank. Found in the wild living in blackwater peat swamps.

NATIVE RANGE: Thailand, Malaysia, West Kalimantan on the Island of Borneo, Sumatra

MAXIMUM SIZE: 1.2 in. (3 cm)

MINIMUM AQUARIUM SIZE: 10 gal. (38 L)

WATER PARAMETERS: pH 5–7.5, 68–77°F (20–25°C)

FEEDING: Micropredator. Readily accepts dried foods, but should be offered a variety that includes *Daphnia* and baby brine shrimp, along with *Cyclops* (dried or frozen) and Golden Pearls, which mimic newly hatched *Artemia*.

BEHAVIOR & CARE: Because of their flexibility with regard to water chemistry, they can be combined with most peaceful community fishes available in the hobby, like danios, rasboras, and *Pangio*. It is also an excellent choice to pair with the more diminutive betta species. They should be kept in a large group, with eight or more being preferred. Their only limiting factor for compatibility is their small size; care must be taken when choosing filtration devices and the sizes of tankmates. Leaf litter is a good addition to a tank housing this species, providing acidity, staining the water dark, and serving as a breeding ground for microorganisms that can feed tiny fry. Java Fern and *Cryptocoryne* spp. can tolerate these water conditions.

GLOWLIGHT DANIO *Danio choprae*

OVERVIEW: The Glowlight Danio, which has only become available in the aquarium trade in the past decade or so, is already a consummate favorite because of its striking coloration at maturity. Most stock available now is captive-bred. With its versatility in terms of water parameters and tight schooling behavior, it is an excellent addition to a hillstream biotope with some water current provided.

NATIVE RANGE: Northern Myanmar

MAXIMUM SIZE: 1.2 in. (3 cm)

MINIMUM AQUARIUM SIZE: 10 gal. (38 L)

WATER PARAMETERS: pH 6–8, 70–80°F (21–27°C)

FEEDING: Micropredator. Readily accepts dried foods, but should be offered variety, including *Cyclops*, bloodworms, *Daphnia*, and baby brine shrimp for best coloring.

BEHAVIOR & CARE: Extremely fast-moving and tightly schooling. Groups of 10 or more are preferred. They like highly oxygenated water, so they are an excellent companion for species like *Stiphodon* and *Rhinogobious*, as well as *Tanichthys*. They can also be housed with most community-type fishes found within the hobby, like livebearers, tetras, rainbow fishes, anabantoids, and *Corydoras* or *Aspidoras* catfishes. In a hillsteam biotope, this fish would be a good companion for the Reticulated Hillstream Loach, *Sewellia lineolata.* They are egg scatterers and exhibit no parental care. They are notorious jumpers, and a tight-fitting top must be provided on the aquarium. This fish should not be confused with the so-called "Glofish," a transgenic product of the laboratory.

EMERALD DWARF RASBORA *Danio erythromicron*
(formerly *Microrasbora erythromicron,* Thick-Band Purple Zebra,
Crossbanded Dwarf Rasbora)

OVERVIEW: With its striking blue vertical barring and red to orange
fins, this little fish is a stunner. It is an excellent choice for a heavily
planted and carefully aquascaped nano-tank.

NATIVE RANGE: Lake Inle, Myanmar

MAXIMUM SIZE: 0.8 in. (2 cm)

MINIMUM AQUARIUM SIZE: 5 gal. (19 L)

WATER PARAMETERS: pH 7–8, 68–75°F (20–24°C)

FEEDING: Micropredator. Readily takes frozen or live foods like
Cyclops, Daphnia, and baby brine shrimp. Offer a varied diet consisting of these and live foods, such as white worms, as well as good
quality flake foods.

BEHAVIOR & CARE: Notoriously skittish, these fish do best on a
dark substrate in a well-planted tank. Most appropriate tankmates
include *Danio choprae, Dario hysginon, Sawbwa resplendens,
Microrasbora rubescens,* and *Petruicthys brevis.* They will often
school with the *Petruichthys* loaches; the Rosy species is closest to
their size. They should not be housed with *Danio margaritatus,* as
there is a risk of hybridization. Boisterous or large tankmates should
be avoided, as they will easily intimidate this small fish. It will jump
from an uncovered aquarium or through narrow openings in the
aquarium top.

CELESTIAL PEARL DANIO *Danio margaritatus*
(CPD, Galaxy Rasbora, Fireworks Rasbora)

OVERVIEW: With a speckled body and bright orange fins, this little gem has taken the fish world by storm, quickly becoming a massive favorite of hobbyists at all levels. Once rumored to be nearly extinct, it has since been found in many locations and is easily farmed and bred domestically.

NATIVE RANGE: Myanmar to Thailand

MAXIMUM SIZE: 0.8 in. (2 cm)

MINIMUM AQUARIUM SIZE: 5 gal. (19 L)

WATER PARAMETERS: pH 6.5–7.5, 68–78°F (20–26°C)

FEEDING: Micropredator. While this fish readily accepts good quality dried flake, a varied diet including microcrustaceans like *Cyclops*, *Daphnia*, baby brine shrimp, and live foods like white or microworms help to keep it in breeding condition.

BEHAVIOR & CARE: This fish can become shy in the presence of larger or boisterous tankmates, though other small cyprinids like *Danio choprae* and *Microdevario kubotai* are suitable. Other similar-sized surface-dwelling species, like Endler's Livebearers, seem to make it more outgoing. It should not be housed with *Danio erythromicron*, as there is a reported risk of hybridization. Males are distinguished by more intense red and black striping in the fins, except for the pectorals. Egg scatterers, they will predate upon their own eggs and fry, although adding dense mats of Java Moss can result in small numbers of fry showing up in the display tank. Mop spawning is the most reliable way of getting high yields of fry.

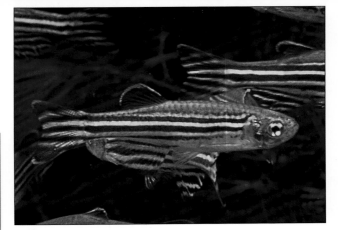

ZEBRA DANIO *Danio rerio*

OVERVIEW: A venerable favorite, the Zebra Danio has been kept by almost all hobbyists at some point. *D. rerio* is available in several color forms, including gold and blue. The Leopard Danio, erroneously referred to as *D. frankei*, is either a color form of *D. rerio* or a hybrid between *D. rerio* and some other *Danio* species. Longfin versions exist for all the color forms. Zebra Danios are a common research subject, and as an offshoot of research into environmental pollutants, a fluorescence gene from marine invertebrates was inserted in an attempt to determine whether a waterway was polluted. Someone realized the commercial potential of these colorful creatures and a new market was created. Love them or hate them, "Glofish" Zebras are here to stay and new colors continue to reach the market. Glofish particularly appeal to children, and if that is what it takes to get kids started with aquariums, let them keep Glofish.

NATIVE RANGE: India

MAXIMUM SIZE: 2 in. (5 cm)

MINIMUM AQUARIUM SIZE: 10 gal. (38 L)

WATER PARAMETERS: pH and hardness unimportant, 70–76°F (21–24°C)

FEEDING: Omnivore. Will eat all prepared foods, but should be offered frozen and live foods on a regular basis.

BEHAVIOR & CARE: They are frenetic, perpetual-motion swimmers. They should be kept in as large a school as possible and only with tankmates that can tolerate their activity level. They spend most of their time near the surface, so their tankmates should be species that live lower in the water column.

GOLD RING DANIO *Danio tinwini*
(Fire Ring Danio, Spotted Danio, Burma Danio)

OVERVIEW: A tiny gold fish with blue spots, it is subtly flashy and an excellent addition to a heavily planted tank. Adaptable in terms of water chemistry and suitable to keep with a wide range of tank-mates, the Gold Ring Danio is an excellent beginner's fish. It should be kept in schools of at least 8 to 10 fish for its own well-being and so that its keeper can observe its natural behaviors.

NATIVE RANGE: Myanmar

MAXIMUM SIZE: 1.2 in. (3 cm)

MINIMUM AQUARIUM SIZE: 5 gal. (19 L)

WATER PARAMETERS: 65–80°F (18–27°C)

FEEDING: Micropredator. A largely unfussy feeder. A range of good quality dried flake and frozen or live white worms, *Daphnia*, *Cyclops*, or baby brine shrimp is preferred.

BEHAVIOR & CARE: A schooling fish by nature, this species should be kept in groups of 8 to 10 or more. Ideal tankmates include *Danio choprae*, *Dario*s, or peaceful community fishes of comparable size like rainbows, tetras, small catfishes, and anabantoids. This fish is an athletic jumper, so the aquarium should have a tightly fitting lid. It is an excellent choice for a nano-aquarium, but if you decide to add it to a larger community tank, avoid keeping it with aggressive species like angelfishes or large gouramis.

DADIO *Laubuca dadiburjori*
(formerly *Chela dadiburjori,* Orange Hatchet Fish, Indian Hatchet Fish)

OVERVIEW: Fairly new to the hobby, this fish is now being spawned commercially and is destined to become an industry staple. In a planted tank with soft water, the orange really glows. Another prominent feature of the color pattern is the black mid-body bar, which sports three slightly larger black spots on most specimens. In ideal lighting, the black bar is overlain with a blue sheen. Females are plumper than males.

NATIVE RANGE: Kerala, India

MAXIMUM SIZE: 1.25 in. (3.2 cm)

MINIMUM AQUARIUM SIZE: 10 gal. (38 L)

WATER PARAMETERS: pH 6–7.5, soft to moderate, 73–79°F (23–26°C)

FEEDING: Carnivore. Feed high quality flakes and pellets supplemented with frozen foods. Feeding live or frozen *Cyclops* and baby brine shrimp will enhance the orange color.

BEHAVIOR & CARE: This is a peaceful, active fish that spends most of its time up in the water column. It shows its best colors in a well-lit, heavily planted aquarium and when maintained in a group of at least five. Keep with other schooling fishes that swim lower in the water column. Like other danionins, it is a well-known jumper, and the aquarium should have a carefully fitted top.

GREEN NEON MICRORASBORA *Microdevario kubotai*
(Kubotai's Rasbora, Yellow Neon Microrasbora)

OVERVIEW: The best-known of the *Microdevario* species, the Green Neon has earned a reputation as a vibrant addition to a nano-tank. Ranging in color from bright neon yellow to a vivid lime green, this is a little fish with a big impact. All microrasboras should be kept in groups of at least 8 to 12 for best behavior and to provide the fish with a sense of security.

NATIVE RANGE: Thailand

MAXIMUM SIZE: 0.8 in. (2 cm)

MINIMUM AQUARIUM SIZE: 5 gal. (19 L)

WATER PARAMETERS: pH 6–7, 71–80°F (22–27°C)

FEEDING: Micropredator. It readily accepts small dried or frozen foods such as *Cyclops*, frozen baby *Artemia*, or *Daphnia*, along with good quality color-enhancing flake foods. Golden Pearls are a convenient, high quality, dried micropellet food for fishes of this size. Feed all small fishes at least twice daily.

BEHAVIOR & CARE: In nature, this fish is found in schools of two dozen or more, and a group of this size in a larger nano-tank would be quite a spectacle. Because of their tiny size, they do best with other fishes of small stature, like those in the genera *Boraras*, *Trigonostigma*, *Dario*, and *Pangio*. Kubotai's Rasbora appreciates well-oxygenated water, areas of planting, and a dark substrate. They should not be housed with fishes much larger than themselves.

DRAPE FIN BARB *Oreichthys crenuchoides*
(*Oreichthys cosuatis* "High Fin," Highfin Neon Barb)

OVERVIEW: Although understated in color, this fish exhibits exceptionally engaging behavior and is a perfect choice for the moderate to advanced hobbyist. Gentle-natured and able to be spawned, this is a great project fish that is uncommon but worth the effort to source. Should be kept in shoals of at least 6 to 10 fish.

NATIVE RANGE: Brahmaputra River, West Bengal, eastern India

MAXIMUM SIZE: 1.7 in. (4.3 cm)

MINIMUM AQUARIUM SIZE: 20 gal. (76 L)

WATER PARAMETERS: pH 6–7.5, 73–82°F (23–28°C)

FEEDING: Micropredator. It will happily take dried foods like good quality flake or pellets, but should be offered a variety, including frozen foods like baby brine shrimp, *Cyclops*, and *Daphnia*.

BEHAVIOR & CARE: Too shy for the large community aquarium, where it would be out-competed for food and swimming space, this fish does great with *Trigonostigma*, *Boraras*, *Brevibora*, and South American characins, as well as *Otocinclus* and *Corydoras* catfishes. They are sexually dimorphic; the male has a long, yellow-checkered dorsal fin, and the female is broader-bodied and has a short yellow dorsal fin with a black tip. This species does best in a well-planted tank with ample floating vegetation to dim the lighting.

CHECKERBOARD BARB *Puntius oligolepis*
(Island Barb, Checker Barb, Checkered Barb)

OVERVIEW: One of the best choices for a nano-tank from this speciose genus. Readily available from breeders in Asia but not always in stock at fish stores. One of the most underrated species in the hobby. What appears to be a drab brown fish in the store turns into something spectacular when acclimated to a well-lit, heavily planted aquarium. Males are more colorful and somewhat smaller than females.

NATIVE RANGE: Island of Sumatra, western Indonesia

MAXIMUM SIZE: 2 in. (5 cm)

MINIMUM AQUARIUM SIZE: 10 gal. (38 L)

WATER PARAMETERS: 6–7.5, moderate hardness, 74–80°F (23–27°C)

FEEDING: Omnivore. Accepts a wide range of dry and frozen foods. Occasional feedings of live food enhance colors. Offer food for small predators as well as mixed rations containing *Spirulina* or other vegetable matter. Color-enhancing flakes should be offered several times a week.

BEHAVIOR & CARE: This species chools very loosely. They should be kept in groups of at least six fish. Males will display to each other and to females, occasionally resulting in a nipped fin but seldom anything more severe. May nip the fins of long-finned, slow-moving species like domestic *Betta*s.

CHERRY BARB *Puntius titteya*

OVERVIEW: Although it is an extremely common and breedable fish, the Cherry Barb is one of the most underrated of all. Both males and females become vividly red and have a very docile behavior, despite their grouping with the barbs, well-known fin nippers in community tanks. These are excellent beginner fish that won't disappoint. Fish shown above is a male in breeding coloration.

NATIVE RANGE: Sri Lanka (at risk of extinction)

MAXIMUM SIZE: 2 in. (5 cm)

MINIMUM AQUARIUM SIZE: 10 gal. (38 L)

WATER PARAMETERS: pH 6–8, 68–80°F (20–27°C)

FEEDING: Omnivore. Pigment-enhancing *Cyclops* and flakes should be offered several times a week. Accepts a wide range of dry and frozen foods. Occasional feedings of live food will help to enhance colors. Offer food for small predators as well as mixed rations containing *Spirulina* or other vegetable matter.

BEHAVIOR & CARE: Undemanding as to water chemistry, Cherry Barbs are a quintessential choice for a planted community tank. Suitable tankmates include tetras, livebearers, rainbows, catfishes, anabantoids, and loaches. Cherry Barbs are widely available and most striking when kept in mixed groups of at least six or eight, with more females than males. Females have a reputation for being drab, but when in breeding dress they acquire a rich red color, almost as vibrant as that of the males.

ASIAN RUMMYNOSE *Sawbwa resplendens*
(Naked Rasbora, Rummynose Rasbora)

OVERVIEW: An absolutely stunning fish when in breeding dress, *Sawbwa resplendens* is a great choice for a small planted tank or Lake Inle biotope tank. Females can be difficult to source but are well worth the effort, as males exhibit their best coloration in a shoal with a mixed gender ratio.

NATIVE RANGE: Lake Inle, Myanmar

MAXIMUM SIZE: 1 in. (2.5 cm)

MINIMUM AQUARIUM SIZE: 5 gal. (19 L)

WATER PARAMETERS: pH 7–8, 65–75°F (18–24°C)

FEEDING: Omnivore. Thrives on a diet of frozen or live small foods like *Daphnia*, *Cyclops*, or baby brine shrimp. Readily accepts good quality flake rations that include ingredients for both carnivores and herbivores.

BEHAVIOR & CARE: This fish shows a strong sexual dimorphism. The females are largely clear to a light lemon yellow color, while the males are a vivid steel blue color with a bright red nose and fin tips. An ideal ratio is at least two males to four females, though this can be difficult to accomplish. It is not an ideal community fish because of its small size and the aggressive nature of sparring males. Ideal tankmates are *Petruichthys brevis* and *Danio erythromicron*, as well as some *Devario* species.

111

NEON BLUE RASBORA *Sundadanio axelrodi*
(Axelrod's Rasbora, Red Neon Rasbora)

OVERVIEW: A blackwater species originating from rainforest peat swamps, this is a species for the advanced hobbyist. Blue Neon Rasbora males are absolutely stunning when in good condition. They do best in a heavily planted tank with driftwood and leaf litter to add tannins.

NATIVE RANGE: Borneo, Sumatra, Indonesia

MAXIMUM SIZE: 0.8 in. (2 cm)

MINIMUM AQUARIUM SIZE: 5 gal. (19 L)

WATER PARAMETERS: pH 4–6.5, 73–79°F (23–26°C)

FEEDING: Micropredator. A mixed diet of baby brine shrimp, *Daphnia*, Grindal or micro-worms, and *Cyclops* is best. They rarely take prepared foods well. Small live foods are important just after import, as the fish are often in poor condition.

BEHAVIOR & CARE: This species exists in several color forms depending on the locality of collection; fish from the south and east are blue or green and western specimens are red or orange. This is a very timid fish, and care should be taken when choosing tankmates. It does well with species like *Trigonostigma*, *Boraras*, small tetras like *H. amandae*, and pencilfishes. A schooling species with a very timid personality, they must be kept in shoals—the larger, the better. A grouping of 20 or more will help bring out their best coloration and behaviors.

WHITE CLOUD MOUNTAIN FISH *Tanichthys albonubes*
(Meteor Minnow, White Cloud Mountain Minnow)

OVERVIEW: White Clouds are the delight of minimalist aquarists. Colorful and very peaceful, these charming little minnows are ideal schooling fish. The long-finned form is generally called the Meteor Minnow. It remained monotypic until 2001, when *T. micagemmae* and *T. thacbaensis* were described from Vietnam. The former has been available for a number of years and is an excellent aquarium fish, though it may be endangered in nature.

NATIVE RANGE: China, Vietnam

MAXIMUM LENGTH: 1.5 in. (4 cm)

WATER: pH 6.0–8.0, hardness 5–19°dGH, 64–72°F (18–22°C)

MINIMUM AQUARIUM SIZE: 15 gal. (57 L)

FEEDING: Micropredator. Eats zooplankton and detritus in the wild. The White Cloud does well on fine prepared foods, frozen brine shrimp, bloodworms, mosquito larvae, and *Cyclops*.

BEHAVIOR & CARE: Once referred to as the "poor man's Neon," this is a versatile fish that can be kept in a variety of water conditions, but it does better in cooler temperatures with good oxygen levels. An excellent candidate for outdoor breeding in temperate seasons, White Clouds are prolific and easy to raise, rarely predating on their eggs or fry if ample leafy plants or mosses are provided. Their vibrant colors, peaceful attitude, and ease of breeding make them an excellent and rewarding choice for aquarists at all levels. They are now available in albino, golden, super-red, and long-finned forms.

SPARKLING GEM MINNOW *Tanichthys micagemmae*
(Vietnamese White Cloud, Sparkling Gem White Cloud)

OVERVIEW: Versatile and attractive, this newly described White Cloud–like minnow is a great addition to the majority of community tanks and an appropriate beginner fish. They are also well suited to breeding outdoors in temperate months. They are sometimes confused with another species named the Vietnamese White Cloud, *Tanichthys thacbaensis*.

NATIVE RANGE: Vietnam

MAXIMUM SIZE: 1.1 in. (2.8 cm)

MINIMUM AQUARIUM SIZE: 5 gal. (19 L)

WATER PARAMETERS: pH 6–7.5, 65–75°F (18–24°C)

FEEDING: Micropredator. Readily accepts most quality dried flakes and pellets, though they appreciate being offered live or frozen foods like baby brine shrimp, *Cyclops*, or *Daphnia*, rotifers, and Golden Pearls, micro-sized pellets that mimic newly hatched *Artemia*.

BEHAVIOR & CARE: Very peaceful, the Sparkling Gem Minnow is an ideal resident for a community tank. It is versatile with its needs, and can easily be put into a stream tank with fishes like *Stiphodons* or *Rhinogobius* or adapted to a more typical setup featuring danios, darios, cyprinids, livebearers, tetras, and catfishes.

LAMBCHOP RASBORA *Trigonostigma espei*
(False Harlequin, Espei Rasbora)

OVERVIEW: With its bright copper color and bold, lambchop-shaped marking, the Espei Rasbora is a popular choice for a carefully aquascaped tank. It is similar to the more common Harlequin Rasbora, *T. heteromorpha*. Easy to maintain and peaceful, it does well in a community tank.

NATIVE RANGE: Thailand, Cambodia

MAXIMUM SIZE: 1.2 in. (3 cm)

MINIMUM AQUARIUM SIZE: 5 gal. (19 L)

WATER PARAMETERS: pH 5–7.5, 72–82°F (22–28°C)

FEEDING: Micropredator. Does best on a mixed diet of quality flake and frozen foods like bloodworms, *Daphnia*, and baby brine shrimp.

BEHAVIOR & CARE: The most boldly colored of this complex, this is a wonderful species for a small planted tank or a large, peaceful community. They appreciate areas of planting and look best over a dark substrate. As with others of similar size, a group of eight or more is best. Appropriate tankmates include many of the most popular fishes in the hobby, including other small cyprinids as well as tetras, livebearers, dwarf cichlids, catfishes, and loaches. Because of its size, care should be taken not to place it with fishes that are too large. *Trigonostigma hengeli* is a similar species, but can be differentiated from the Lambchop because the majority of the body is colorless, sometimes with a yellow to light orange pigmentation, with a pronounced neon stripe along the lampchop-shaped black marking.

HARLEQUIN RASBORA *Trigonostigma heteromorpha*
(Harlequin)

OVERVIEW: This beautiful species is a wonderful addition to a larger nano-aquarium. It has an unusual spawning methodology for a cyprinid, laying eggs on the undersides of leaves in a somewhat cichlid-like fashion. In typical cyprinid fashion, no parental care of the eggs or fry is practiced. Most specimens sold are aquacultured, and some lack the vivid colors of wild-caught fish. The Singapore wild population is endangered by deforestation and overcollecting for the aquarium trade.

NATIVE RANGE: Thailand, Malaysia, Sumatra, Singapore
MAXIMUM SIZE: 2 in. (5 cm)
MINIMUM AQUARIUM SIZE: 15 gal. (57 L)
WATER PARAMETERS: pH 6.5–7.5, 70–78°F (21–26°C); requires water with a high oxygen content.
FEEDING: Readily accepts all prepared foods. Offer a varied diet including dry, frozen, and live foods. Live baby brine shrimp are a particular favorite.
BEHAVIOR & CARE: This species does best in a group of 7 to 12 fish, and the bigger the group, the better. As with many species, keeping a group of mixed sexes helps bring out the best color displays. It spends most of its time in the middle to high part of the water column, so it's a great choice for tall aquariums and works well when stocked with a surface-hugging species like the Marble Hatchet (*Carnegiella strigata*) to add another level of movement. The related species *T. espei* and *T. hengeli* share the behavior but don't grow as large.

116

SCARLET GOBY *Rhinogobius zhoui*
(Flame Goby, Chinese Vermilion Goby)

OVERVIEW: Though expensive, this fish is a great acquisition for the advanced hobbyist and worth every penny. They are full of personality and can be bred in fresh water. They make a stunning impact in a display tank, although it may be difficult to find a source of stock.

NATIVE RANGE: Guandong Province, China

MAXIMUM SIZE: 1.4 in. (3.5 cm)

MINIMUM AQUARIUM SIZE: 10 gal. (38 L)

WATER PARAMETERS: pH 7–7.8, 66–75°F (19–24°C)

FEEDING: Carnivore. This fish is very prey-driven and prefers live foods like white worms, baby brine shrimp, or other appropriately sized worms. Readily eats dwarf livebearer fry and dwarf shrimp, and can be supplemented with frozen bloodworms.

BEHAVIOR & CARE: In most cases, it is best to keep these fish in a species tank with an equal number of males and females. Setup should include many sizes of small rocks with areas of stacked structure. Sturdy rhizome plants can be added for interest, but they are not necessary for this species. High oxygen and exceptionally clear water is required, though directional flow is not very important. Adult males tend to be significantly brighter in color, having extended, unpaired fins with a bright bluish tint to the edges. While a species tank is recommended, they could also be kept with fishes that inhabit the top portion of the water column, like *Tanichthys* or *Microdevario* species. Small invertebrates and fishes should be avoided because of the strong predatory tendencies of this fish.

BLUE NEON GOBY *Stiphodon atropurureus*
(Cobalt Blue Goby, Freshwater Neon Goby)

OVERVIEW: A little goby that can show an extremely wide range of colors and patterns based on dominance and gender, these rare gems require a specialized setup of a mature tank with plentiful algae growth and a high level of oxygenation. It is an advanced hobbyist's nano fish, worth every ounce of effort to maintain. A very similar species is *Stiphodon percnopterygionus.*

NATIVE RANGE: Philippines, islands in the South China Sea

MAXIMUM SIZE: 2 inches (5 cm)

MINIMUM AQUARIUM SIZE: 20 gallons (76 L)

WATER PARAMETERS: pH 6.5-7.5; Temperature 60-68; needs clear water with high oxygen content.

FEEDING: Obligate *aufwuchs* grazer. Eats only algae and micro crustaceans. Can be supplemented with specialized gelatinized foods heavy in algae content.

BEHAVIOR & CARE: Must have a high-capacity filter and additional oxygenating aids, prefeably a powerhead pump to create a riverine environment. While they are small of stature, they have big personalities and sparring between males is extremely common. A female-heavy ratio in a species tank is preferred, and with ample space a large colony can be housed. The tank should have stacked rock work and minimal planting, plants like *Bolbitis* and *Anubias* usually work out well. Tank mates should be chosen with care. *Atyoida pilipes*, *Caridina*, and *Neocaridina* shrimp as well as *Neritina* snails are excellent choices as well as small fishes like *Sewellia*, *Tanichthys*, Endler's Livebearers, or Danios. Larger fish are best omitted.

PEACOCK GOBY *Tateurndina ocellicauda*
(Peacock Gudgeon)

OVERVIEW: One of the more colorful small fishes available in the hobby, Peacock Gobies utilize all levels of the tank and are an excellent addition to the heavily planted community aquarium. A good choice for the hobbyist interested in spawning fish.

NATIVE RANGE: Papau New Guinea

MAXIMUM SIZE: 3 in. (8 cm)

MINIMUM AQUARIUM SIZE: 10 gal. (38 L)

WATER PARAMETERS: pH 6.5–7.5, 72–79°F (22–26°C)

FEEDING: Micropredator. Readily accepts dried foods, but should be offered variety including brine shrimp, bloodworms, *Daphnia*, and *Cyclops*.

BEHAVIOR & CARE: Generally peaceful fish, they can squabble amongst themselves, especially during spawning. Males develop a nuchal hump and are larger than females, which also develop a yellow belly when in breeding dress. They tend to breed in caves, so coconut shells, stacked driftwood, or PVC pipes should be provided. During breeding, the male traps the female in a cave, where she deposits her eggs on the ceiling. The male guards the eggs until they hatch, at which time parental care ceases and the fry should be removed so they do not get eaten. A species tank is best for breeding, but they are compatible with rainbow fishes, tetras, rasboras, and *Corydoras* cats, as well as most other comparably sized community fishes. Avoid keeping them with other species that can become territorial during spawning, like dwarf cichlids.

LYRETAIL KILLIFISH *Aphyosemion australe*
(Lyretail Panchax, Chocolate Lyretail, Cape Lopez Lyretail)

OVERVIEW: This fish is available in several color forms, each of which goes by its own common name: Albino Australe, Gold Australe, Orange Australe, Chocolate Australe, and others. Native to small forest streams in Africa. Scatters its eggs in plants or spawning mops. Eggs are water-incubated. The first fish in the hobby were collected on Cape Lopez in Gabon.

NATIVE RANGE: Cameroon to Angola

MAXIMUM SIZE: 2.5 in. (6.4 cm)

MINIMUM AQUARIUM SIZE: 5 gal. (19 L)

WATER PARAMETERS: pH 6–7.5, moderate hardness, 68–76°F (20–24°C)

FEEDING: Carnivore. Live foods preferred, including wingless fruit flies, *Daphnia*, mosquito larvae, *Cyclops*, tropical redworms cut to size, Grindal worms, brine shrimp, etc. Some specimens will accept frozen or dried foods, but these should not constitute a large part of the diet.

BEHAVIOR & CARE: Somewhat shy, though males will fight with each other. Males are more colorful and slightly larger, and have the lyretail that the species is known for. The species does best in a dimly lit planted aquarium. Do not keep with aggressive tankmates that might intimidate it. If not kept in a species tank, good choices for companions are peaceful catfishes, small rasboras, and small tetras. They will occasionally nip the fins of long-finned species. Like other killifishes, this is an accomplished leaper, so a tight-fitting cover is essential.

CLOWN KILLIFISH *Epiplatys annulatus*
(Rocket Killifish, Banded Panchax)

OVERVIEW: With tail colors and a lamp eye that glows, this diminutive species is an absolute stunner and a great choice for the avid aquarist who wants an achievable breeding project. Best kept in a species tank, in groups of two males to four females or comparable ratios. Males are more colorful, with bright blue, red, and yellow striping on their anal fins (depending on locality). Males have longer, more extended fins.

NATIVE RANGE: Southern Guinea to Liberia

MAXIMUM SIZE: 1.4 in. (3.5 cm)

MINIMUM AQUARIUM SIZE: 5 gal. (19 L)

WATER PARAMETERS: pH 4–7, 68–78°F (20–26°C)

FEEDING: Micropredator. While it readily accepts dried foods like flake or micropellets, a varied diet of live white worms, frozen baby brine, *Cyclops*, and *Daphnia* is ideal.

BEHAVIOR & CARE: Relatively easy to breed in a well decorated, mature tank. Floating plants or dense areas of moss near the tank's surface are best to collect eggs. Adults do not predate on the young, but older fry will predate on younger fry when they can. If attempting to set up a community tank, small tetras, cyprinids, anabantoids, and loricariids of similar size and temperament are best. As with all killifishes, a tight-fitting lid is important.

FLORIDA FLAG FISH *Jordanella floridae*
(Flag Fish, American Flag Fish)

OVERVIEW: Here is proof that native American fishes can be both colorful and interesting. This Florida native killifish lives in ponds, lakes, and slow-moving stretches of small rivers and is easy to breed in heavily planted aquariums. It is very hardy and tolerant of different water conditions, and occasionally enters brackish water in the wild. Spawns in plants or in a nest built by the male in the substrate. The male is more colorful and slightly larger, and guards the nest after spawning.

NATIVE RANGE: Florida

MAXIMUM SIZE: 2.25 in. (6 cm)

MINIMUM AQUARIUM SIZE: 5 gal. (19 L)

WATER PARAMETERS: pH 7–8, moderately hard to hard, 70–76°F (21–24°C)

FEEDING: Omnivore. Feeds on crustaceans, insects, worms, and algae. Readily accepts flakes, pellets, and frozen foods. Live food should be included in the diet.

BEHAVIOR & CARE: This is a somewhat territorial species that behaves more like cichlids than most other killifishes. Should be kept in pairs or with more females than males. Does best in a dimly lit planted aquarium with schools of upper-water dwellers as tank-mates. White Clouds and danios are particularly good choices. Java Moss and Marimo Balls will serve as ideal spawning sites. It is an interesting choice for a seasonal outdoor water garden or a small pond, where it will multiply in numbers over the summer months.

BLUEFIN NOTHO *Nothobranchius rachovii*
(Rachov's Notho)

OVERVIEW: Like other *Nothobranchius* spp., this is an annual killifish that lives in seasonal pools. To survive, annual killies lay their eggs in the mud at the bottoms of the pools. When the rains come and the pools fill, the eggs hatch and a new generation is born. The typical form of the Bluefin Notho, which just might be the world's most beautiful fish, was collected around Beira, Mozambique. Hobbyists looking for this fish should purchase *N. rachovii* "Beira 98," which represents the progeny from a more recent collection than the more common aquarium strain.

NATIVE RANGE: Mozambique

MAXIMUM SIZE: 2.25 in. (6 cm)

MINIMUM AQUARIUM SIZE: 2 gal. (8 L)

WATER PARAMETERS: pH 6.5–8, moderately hard to hard, 70–78°F (21–26°C)

FEEDING: Carnivore. Live foods should form the staple diet. *Daphnia*, mosquito larvae, baby brine shrimp, bloodworms, Grindal worms, etc. should be fed with as much variety as possible. Small amounts of frozen or dried food may be accepted.

BEHAVIOR & CARE: Males are aggressive toward each other and will drive females very hard. The best situation is one male with as many females as possible. In a community setting, a single male is probably the best choice. Will nip the fins of long-finned and slow-moving species. The colors show best in a planted tank with dim lighting. This species is very susceptible to velvet, so be on the lookout for it.

NORMAN'S LAMPEYE *Poropanchax normani*
(Blue Eye Killifish)

OVERVIEW: This is a glittery little fish that can make a delightful display in a nano-aquarium. It is a schooling, mop-spawning species and one of the most readily available killies in the aquarium trade. It is regularly captive-bred in Asia, and an albino form is occasionally offered.

NATIVE RANGE: Western and central Africa

MAXIMUM SIZE: 1.6 in. (4 cm)

MINIMUM AQUARIUM SIZE: 5 gal. (19 L)

WATER PARAMETERS: Not important, 74–78°F (23–26°C)

FEEDING: Carnivore. Feeds on aquatic crustaceans and insect larvae in the wild, and the captive diet should replicate this. Dry and frozen foods are readily taken and live food should be fed whenever possible. Good choices include *Cyclops*, baby brine shrimp, *Daphnia*, and Golden Pearls, dried micropellets designed to mimic the movements of floating newly hatched *Artemia*.

BEHAVIOR & CARE: Easy to maintain and very peaceful, Norman's Lampeye shows its colors to best advantage in moderately lit, well-planted aquariums. The body color is subtle, yet attractive, and the eye is a real attention-getter. Keep in as large a group as possible with similarly sized peaceful species. Add a school of more colorful fishes, such as Cardinal Tetras, to inhabit the lower reaches of the tank, and some anabantoids to cross all water levels. In a deep tank, a school of hatchets will add some nice surface movement above the lampeyes.

SWAMP GUPPY *Micropoecilia picta*
(Scarlet Livebearer)

OVERVIEW: The Swamp Guppies, *Micropoecilia* spp., are active, delightful little fishes and represent a challenging group of livebearers for the advanced hobbyist. *M. picta,* shown above, *and M. parae* both occur naturally in several color forms, while *M. branneri* all look pretty much the same. Females are larger than males, but males have most of the color.

NATIVE RANGE: Brazil to Trinidad

MAXIMUM SIZE: 2 in. (5 cm)

MINIMUM AQUARIUM SIZE: 10 gal. (38 L)

WATER PARAMETERS: pH 7–8.5, hard to slightly brackish, 74–78°F (23–26°C)

FEEDING: Omnivore. Feed a mix of dry foods for both carnivores and herbivores and supplement that with frozen and live foods, including brine shrimp, *Daphnia*, and *Cyclops*.

BEHAVIOR & CARE: *M. parae* and *M. picta* are coastal species that venture into brackish water; *M. branneri* comes from further inland. The addition of some salt, up to 1 tablespoon per 2 gallons (7.5 L), can be beneficial, particularly if they seem stressed. *M. parae* and *M. picta* are commercially bred in small numbers. *M. branneri*, on the other hand, seems to only be available as a wild-caught fish. Regardless of their origin, these fish do not ship well, so quarantine is necessary. They should be treated very gently until they've fully acclimated to your water conditions. Species aquariums are best to maximize breeding, but they are suitable for community settings with small, non-aggressive species.

GUPPY *Poecilia reticulata*
(Million Fish)

OVERVIEW: Probably the world's best-known aquarium fish, the Guppy is both a hardy beginner's species and the object of passionate breeding efforts to produce ever more spectacular color forms. It is a highly prolific livebearer, available in a dazzling array of color and finnage variations. Females are larger than males and generally less colorful. Having both sexes almost guarantees fry. Widely introduced in tropical regions to control mosquitoes in the first half of the twentieth century, it is considered an invasive species in many areas. Many of the fancy varieties are commercially raised with a heavy salt concentration to alleviate disease issues. Such specimens don't always fare well in pure fresh water.

NATIVE RANGE: Northeast South America and southern Caribbean, notably Venezuela, Trinidad, Tobago, Barbados

MAXIMUM SIZE: 2.5 in. (6 cm)

MINIMUM AQUARIUM SIZE: 5 gal. (19 L)

WATER PARAMETERS: pH 7–8, hard, 70–78°F (21–26°C)

FEEDING: Omnivore. Accepts all typical aquarium foods. Use a specialized guppy food as a staple diet and supplement with frozen foods and live baby brine shrimp and other small live foods.

BEHAVIOR & CARE: The wild-type fish are a particularly good choice for beginners. Highly bred forms are more susceptible to diseases and more demanding of high water quality. Tankmates should be peaceful with no fin nippers. Adding up to a tablespoon of salt per 2 gallons (7.5 L) can be beneficial. Keep more than one female for each male so the females get a chance to rest a bit.

ENDLER'S LIVEBEARER *Poecilia wingei*
(Endler's Guppy)

OVERVIEW: Closely related to but distinct from the Guppy, this nano-livebearer is full of energy and displays flashy colors. Will mate with Guppies, and many of the new color forms that are sold as varieties of *P. wingei* are actually hybrids. May be extinct in the wild. Line breeding and selectively breeding to encourage particular color patterns, along with hybridization with guppies, threatens to eventually result in the loss of the original wild pattern. Males are much more colorful and much smaller than females.

NATIVE RANGE: Native to warm lakes, northeastern Venezuela

MAXIMUM SIZE: Males 1 in. (2.5 cm), females 1.75 in. (4.5 cm)

MINIMUM AQUARIUM SIZE: 5 gal. (19 L)

WATER PARAMETERS: pH 7–8.5, hard, 75–82°F (24–28°C)

FEEDING: Omnivore. Does well on a diet of dry foods intended for guppies. Some plant-based dry food should be included. Frozen foods such as *Daphnia* and brine shrimp should also be fed. Endler's benefits from the inclusion of small live foods, such as baby brine shrimp and color-enhancing *Cyclops*.

BEHAVIOR & CARE: Colorful and active, this is a wonderful nano-aquarium species. When found in pet shops, it is frequently only the more colorful males that are available. If breeding is not desired, adding males only will give a nice pop of color to any tank with at least moderate water hardness. Prefers planted aquariums with small, peaceful tankmates, such as tetras, rasboras, labyrinth fishes, and Corydoradinae catfishes.

PLATY *Xiphophorus maculatus, X. variatus*

OVERVIEW: While typically listed as distinct species in the aquarium literature, all the Platies in the aquarium hobby are hybrids, having been crossed with each other as well as the swordtail *Xiphophorus helleri*, and possibly other species of *Xiphophorus*, to develop the myriad of color strains and finnage types available today. Fish with a more elongated, slender body are referred to as *X. variatus*, while the fish called *X. maculatus* are chunkier and deeper-bodied. Hardy and prolific, these are excellent beginners' fish. To avoid fry production, add only males. Males are smaller than females and can be distinguished by the modification of the anal fin into a gonopodium used to impregnate the females.

NATIVE RANGE: Central America. *X. maculatus*: Mexico to Belize. *X. variatus*: Mexico

MAXIMUM SIZE: 2.5 in. (6.4 cm)

MINIMUM AQUARIUM SIZE: 10 gal. (38 L)

WATER PARAMETERS: Platies are not particular, but they tend to do best in hard, alkaline water, 72–78°F (22–26°C)

FEEDING: Omnivore. Feed a variety of dry foods for both carnivores and herbivores. Add some frozen and live foods, such as brine shrimp and *Daphnia*, with regular feeding of pigment-enhancing dry flakes containing carotenoids to boost their red and yellow hues.

BEHAVIOR & CARE: If keeping in a mixed sex group, add more females than males. These are active fish that will graze some algae. Do not keep with shy fish or they will out-compete them at feeding time.

DWARF CHAIN LOACH *Ambastaia sidthimunki*
(formerly Botia Sidthimunki; Sid Loach, Dwarf Botia, Chipmunk Botia)

OVERVIEW: These vibrant and mild-tempered little loaches make an excellent community addition to a larger planted nano-tank. Like many of the loaches, these fish thrive in large groups; eight or more is ideal. The Dwarf Chain Loach was once a highly prized rarity, but commercial aquaculture now makes captive-bred specimens readily available and much more affordable.

NATIVE RANGE: Thailand

MAXIMUM SIZE: 2.2 in. (6 cm)

MINIMUM AQUARIUM SIZE: 20 gal. (76 L)

WATER PARAMETERS: pH 6–7.5, 75–86°F (24–30°C)

FEEDING: Micropredator. Readily accepts small frozen foods like *Cyclops* or *Daphnia*. They can be supplemented with small meaty pellets or flake. Offerings of live white worms are appreciated. They will eat pest snails and shrimp in the home aquarium.

BEHAVIOR & CARE: The smallest of the Botiine loach group, this species is often found shoaling (swimming in non-synchronized clusters) in mid-water during daylight hours. The aquarium should have soft, sandy substrate, driftwood, plants, and a moderate amount of water flow. Suitable tankmates include danios, rasboras, and devarios. Fishes with long fins and those that are particularly slow-moving should be avoided. Unfortunately, this fish is considered threatened in the wild, and according to the highly informative SeriouslyFish.com, "Thai localities are kept secret for conservation purposes." Captive-bred specimens are recommended.

HOVERING ZEBRA LOACH *Micronemacheilus cruciatus*
(formerly *Yunnanilus cruciatus*; Dwarf Zebra Hovering Loach,
Vietnamese Multi-Banded Loach, Laos Pygmy Loach)

OVERVIEW: A petite yet gregarious loach, this is a great choice for a small, densely planted tank. They are very active, making use of the entire water column. A social species, they should be kept in groups of six or more and are often found dancing along the front glass with their typical hovering "loach dance" movements. **NATIVE RANGE:** Vietnam

MAXIMUM SIZE: 1.6 in. (4 cm)

MINIMUM AQUARIUM SIZE: 5 gal. (19 L)

WATER PARAMETERS: pH 6.5–8, 68–78°F (20–26°C)

FEEDING: Micropredator. Readily accepts small frozen foods like *Cyclops, Daphnia,* and baby *Artemia.* They can be supplemented with small, meaty pellets or flake. Offerings of live white worms are appreciated.

BEHAVIOR & CARE: Water should be well oxygenated, but not turbulent. This loach is peaceful and surprisingly bold for its size, and is best paired with species like *Boraras, Microdevario, Trigonostigma, Tanichthys, Microrasboras,* or even small *Hyphessobrycon.* Females are noticeably rounder-bellied than males, though that is the extent of their sexual dimorphism. They will spawn often in a densely planted aquarium, though most fry will be victims of predation unless they are removed to a safer growout aquarium. Some may occasionally survive in a tank with heavy plant cover.

KUHLI LOACH *Pangio myersi, P. semicincta*
(Coolie Loach, Giant Kuhli Loach, Slimy Myer's Loach)

OVERVIEW: Several similar-looking species are sold as Kuhli loaches, but the true *P. kuhlii* is probably not in the hobby. These banded, worm-like or eel-like fish are highly nocturnal and spend much of their time buried in the substrate during the day, so they are seldom seen by the hobbyist. In the wild, these species live in soft-bottomed, slow-moving bodies of water, where they are frequently found in leaf litter. They feed by sifting the substrate to catch small crustaceans, insect larvae, and worms, but they also ingest some organic detritus.

NATIVE RANGE: *P. myersi*: lower Mekong basin, Laos, Cambodia, Vietnam, Thailand. *P. semicincta*: Malaysia, Borneo, Sumatra

MAXIMUM SIZE: 4 in. (10 cm)

MINIMUM AQUARIUM SIZE: 10 gal. (38 L)

WATER PARAMETERS: Highly adaptable; soft and acidic in nature, but also do well in hard, alkaline water in captivity, 72–78°F (22–26°C).

FEEDING: Omnivore. Accepts most flakes and micropellets and frozen foods. Live micro-worms, Grindal worms, baby brine shrimp, and *Daphnia* may coax them out of hiding.

BEHAVIOR & CARE: A soft, smooth, sandy substrate is important so that they can dive into it without scratching themselves on sharp edges. Dim lighting is beneficial and will encourage them to be out and about more. Kuhli loaches are escape artists that require a tight-fitting lid. If undergravel filters are used, they will go down the lift tubes and live under the filter.

ROSY LOACH *Petruichthys* sp. "Rosy"
(*Yunnanilus* sp. "Rosy," *Yunnanilus* sp. "Orange," "*Tuberoschistura arakensis*," Burmese Pink Loach)

OVERVIEW: A petite, yet gregarious loach, the Rosy Loach is a great choice for a small, densely planted tank. They are very active, making use of the entire water column. They are collected in the same waters as the Celestial Pearl Danio, *Danio margaritatus*, and often school with these small danios.

NATIVE RANGE: Myanmar to Northern Thailand

MAXIMUM SIZE: 1 in. (3 cm)

MINIMUM AQUARIUM SIZE: 5 gal. (19 L)

WATER PARAMETERS: pH 6.5-8, 68-78°F (20-26°C)

FEEDING: Micropredator. Accepts small frozen foods like *Cyclops*, *Daphnia*, and baby brine shrimp. They can be supplemented with small, meaty pellets or flake. Offerings of live white worms are readily appreciated.

BEHAVIOR & CARE: Water should be well oxygenated, but not turbulent. It is peaceful and surprisingly bold for its small size, and is best when paired with species like *Boraras*, *Microdevario*, *Trigonostigma*, *Tanichthys*, *Microrasboras*, or even small *Hyphessobrycon*. Loaches should be kept in groups of 8 to 10 or more, otherwise they are noticeably less outgoing. When in breeding dress, males have a long, lateral black stripe and a vivid pink to red coloration. Females have spotting across the entire body, and can be difficult to obtain.

In the pair shown above, the fish in the foreground is the obvious male, displaying the coloration that earns this species its common name.

RETICULATED HILLSTREAM LOACH *Sewellia lineolata*
(Tiger Hillstream Loach, Gold Ring Butterfly Sucker, Vietnamese Hillstream Loach)

OVERVIEW: Introduced to the pet trade in the mid-2000s, this personable little loach has swiftly become popular within the hobby because of its striking patterns and its ability to be bred. Comes from shallow, fast-moving streams with high oxygenation, so a mature aquarium with some water movement and algae growth is required for this species.

NATIVE RANGE: Vietnam

MAXIMUM LENGTH: 2.5 in. (6.4 cm)

MINIMUM AQUARIUM SIZE: 20 gal. (76 L)

WATER: pH 6.5–7.5, hardness 5–15°dGH; 68–75°F (20–24°C)

FEEDING: Aufwuchs (algal turf) grazer. Algae, microcrustaceans, or specialized gelatinized foods are required for this species to thrive.

BEHAVIOR & CARE: Fast, well-aerated water is the order of the day with all hillstream loaches, as they cling to rocks with suction from modified ventral fins. Use fine sand and various sizes of pebbles and rocks for the substrate and decor. Bright light promotes desirable algae growth and, while plants are not required, they can be beneficial to water quality. The most aggressive of the "sucker type" loaches, they are not generally aggressive toward species that look different from themselves. Appropriate tankmates include *Tanichthys*, *Stiphodons*, *Rhinogobius*, *Akysis* and *Hara* catfishes, and fan filtering species of shrimp like *Atyoida pilipes*. Avoid keeping them with similarly shaped fishes, as they can be territorial.

THREADFIN RAINBOWFISH *Iriatherina werneri*
(Featherfin Rainbow)

OVERVIEW: This somewhat sensitive little rainbowfish species is best suited for aquarists with some experience. The male's finnage is truly striking, and the dorsal and anal fin filaments can easily extend beyond the caudal extensions. The males flash their fins to each other to establish dominance and to the females to attract spawning partners. They form shoals in nature, and they are best kept in groups of six to eight, preferably with at least three males and at least five females to fully appreciate this behavior.

NATIVE RANGE: Cape York Peninsula, northern Australia, and southern New Guinea

MAXIMUM SIZE: 1.6 in. (4 cm)

MINIMUM AQUARIUM SIZE: 20 gal. (76 L)

WATER PARAMETERS: pH 6–7.5, soft to moderate, 74–78°F (23–26°C)

FEEDING: Small, live foods such as live brine shrimp, vinegar eels, micro-worms, and Grindal worms are best as a staple food, supplemented with dry and frozen foods.

BEHAVIOR & CARE: The colors show best in moderately lit aquariums with live plants and dark substrates. Floating plants to provide shady areas will be much appreciated. Leave some open areas for swimming and displaying. Be very careful to avoid any potential finnippers when choosing tankmates. Appropriate tankmates include *Microdevario*, *Boraras*, *Trigonostigma*, *Paracheirodon*, pygmy *Corydoras*, *Otocinclus*, and dwarf shrimp.

NEON DWARF RAINBOWFISH *Melanotaenia praecox*
(Neon Rainbow)

OVERVIEW: Although most *Melanotaenia* species grow too large, this beautiful smaller species is very well suited to planted nano-aquariums. Active and robust, it makes a great tankmate for smaller cichlids. Males are slightly more colorful and sport slightly elongated, pointed dorsal and anal fins. Color in the unpaired fins can range from yellow to red. Red, the wild color, is greatly preferred. Typical of *Melanotaenia*, the body deepens with age, particularly in males. *Melanotaenia* prefer hard water and are generally easier to keep than the related Blue-Eyes (*Pseudomugil* spp.).

NATIVE RANGE: Mamberamo River, Irian Jaya, Papua New Guinea

MAXIMUM SIZE: 3 in. (8 cm)

MINIMUM AQUARIUM SIZE: 15 gal. (57 L)

WATER PARAMETERS: pH 6.8–8, moderate to hard, 74–80°F (23–27°C)

FEEDING: Omnivore. Feed a varied diet of flakes and appropriately sized pellets, along with frozen and live foods—brine shrimp and *Cyclops* help to enhance the red color.

BEHAVIOR & CARE: Best kept in a school with multiple members of both sexes. Males will show off to other males and display to females. This species spawns readily by scattering eggs in plants, usually in the morning. In a community setting, this makes for an extra feeding for the rest of the tank. Colors show best in a well lit, heavily planted tank, but be sure to leave plenty of open swimming space.

FORKTAIL BLUE-EYE *Pseudomugil furcatus*
(Furcata Rainbowfish, Forktail Rainbow)

OVERVIEW: Bright yellow fins and striking blue eyes make this small rainbow an excellent choice for someone interested in setting up a planted display or a breeding project. They are readily available in the trade and sexually dimorphic, so it is easy to make sure you get sexed groupings. Fish in the aquarium trade are virtually all captive-bred specimens. Members of this genus are shoaling species and should be kept in groups of at least 6 to 8 fish.

NATIVE RANGE: Musa and Kwagila River basins, Papua New Guinea

MAXIMUM SIZE: 2 in. (5 cm)

MINIMUM AQUARIUM SIZE: 15 gal. (57 L)

WATER PARAMETERS: pH 7–8, 75–82°F (24–28°C)

FEEDING: Micropredator. *Daphnia*, micro-worms, *Cyclops*, or baby brine shrimp are best, though they are easily supplemented with good quality flake food.

BEHAVIOR & CARE: Best kept in a densely planted tank, these fish do appreciate well-oxygenated water with a degree of flow. They are compatible with fishes of comparable size and disposition, specifically cyprinids, gobiids, and smaller melanotaeniids. For best results in breeding, a species tank is recommended and should have dense areas of moss to promote the growth of infusoria and give ample places for fry to hide. Higher yield is maintained with a separate fry tank. Similar species include *Pseudomugil paskai*, and *Pseudomugil conniea*, and *Pseudomugil gertrudae*, opposite.

SPOTTED BLUE-EYE *Pseudomugil gertrudae*
(Gertrudae Blue-Eye, Gertrude's Rainbow, Blue-Eye Spotted Rainbow)

OVERVIEW: One of only two members of the genus exhibiting dark spots in the anal, dorsal, and caudal fins, these miniature rainbow-fishes are a striking and vibrant addition to a heavily planted and carefully aquascaped tank. Easy to breed and maintain, they are an excellent choice for the enthusiast interested in spawning fish. The fish shown here are two *P. gertrudae* "Aru" males displaying.

NATIVE RANGE: Northern Australia, southern New Guinea, and the Aru Islands

MAXIMUM SIZE: 1.5 in. (4 cm)

MINIMUM AQUARIUM SIZE: 15 gal. (57 L)

WATER PARAMETERS: pH 4.5–7.5, 70–82°F (21–28°C)

FEEDING: Micropredator. Should be offered varied live foods like baby brine shrimp, *Daphnia*, and micro-worms, but will readily accept flake foods.

BEHAVIOR & CARE: Domestic strains are undemanding, but depending on where they are collected, blackwater may be required for wild fish. It is easy to mop-spawn these egg scatterers, though they will predate on both their eggs and their young, so a separate tank is recommended for rearing fry. Males are noticeably more colorful and have extended unpaired fins. Best kept in shoals of eight or more with fishes of a similar size and disposition, as they can be a bit timid. They are a good candidate to be housed with dwarf shrimp, though they may predate on the youngest baby shrimp.

"Unknown Way," an Aquatic Gardeners Association winning nano-aquascape created by Leandro Artioli of Brazil, holds just 14 gallons (54 L) and is stocked with a shoal of 20 Green Neon Tetras, Paracheirodon simulans.

Aquascaping choices for smaller aquariums

Most of the plants we keep in aquariums spend the majority of their time growing in marshes or swamps or along riverbanks in the wild and only spend part of their time completely submerged when the water level rises. These species all depend in large part on obtaining nutrients through their roots. While growing submersed, they also absorb nutrients through their leaves.

Fertilizing both the substrate and the water is therefore important for long-term success with aquarium plants. Iron-rich clays such as laterite can be added to the substrate or one of the newer "planted aquarium" substrates with slow-release plant nutrients can be chosen. A general purpose liquid plant fertilizer from any reputable aquarium company should be sufficient for the plants included here. The problem with liquid fertilizers is that the dosing instructions for most of them indicate that they should be used once a week or every other week. Don't follow those instructions. The problem is that this adds more nutrients than the plants can utilize in a very short period of time so those nutrients are available to algae. A better approach is to figure out the dosage for your aquarium and if it is suggested as a weekly dose, divide it into 7 doses. Add 1/7th of the weekly dose per day. Feed the plants every day to keep the system nutrient poor. In this environment, the plants will outcompete the algae for nutrients and you should have few, if any, problems with unwanted algae growth. Careful observation will let the plants themselves tell you how much to dose. The idea is to maximize plant growth while minimizing algae growth. The same holds true for lighting, as previously discussed.

The plants included in this volume have been selected for their hardiness and adaptability. Many others are available for experimentation. Ideal water conditions are listed but most will tolerate conditions outside that range. If your plants are not doing well and you're sure that they have enough iron available, the problem is probably lack of carbon. Carbon can be added in the form of CO_2 and there are numerous approaches to this, including inexpensive cartridge dosing kits that perform very well for many aquarists.

MOSS BALL *Aegagropila linnaeii*
(commonly referred to as *Cladophora prolifera* or *C. aegagropila*, Marimo, Tribbles)

OVERVIEW: Unusual species whose growth form is a ball shape. Think dense aquatic tumbleweed and you'll get a pretty good idea. This is a decorative algae. There are anecdotal reports that the presence of a moss ball will prevent the growth of other algae in the aquarium. This may be true in some situations but is certainly not always the case.

HABITAT: Shallow areas of lakes.

NATIVE RANGE: Europe and Asia.

LIGHTING: Prefers medium to high light but tolerates low light.

WATER: Adaptable to wide pH range, prefers moderately hard to hard water, 67-80°F (19-27°C).

PROPAGATION: Division.

NOTES: Moss balls can literally be dropped into the tank and allowed to settle where they will. Alternatively, they can be wedged into a location where the current won't move them. Moss balls tend to build up some detritus on and inside them. They should be rinsed out when doing water changes. Dip them into the bucket of water that has been removed from the tank and shake them around to remove detritus then gently squeeze them out a few times. In bright light, oxygen bubbles may form on the ball causing it to float.

Anubias barteri var. nana

AFRICAN SPEARHEAD *Anubias barteri*

OVERVIEW: Members of the genus *Anubias* have long been popular with aquarists. In particular, *A. barteri*, with its wide range of natural variants and hobbyist-produced cultivars, provides several plants of real value to nano hobbyists. Anubias grows in a creeping form with the leaves and holdfasts growing out of a rhizome. Make sure you do not bury the rhizome. Anubias can be readily grown on driftwood or rocks. Tie the plant loosely to the surface you want it to grow upon with some nylon fishing line. The plant's holdfasts will grab onto the driftwood or rock fairly quickly. Be sure to point the growing tip in the direction you want the plant to grow. These are slow-growing species that can become covered in algae when excess nutrients and/or light are present in the aquarium. An excellent choice for low-light setups.

HABITAT: Streamside, or sometimes in dry areas among waterfalls

NATIVE RANGE: West Africa

LIGHTING: Highly adaptable. Low to high lighting is acceptable.

WATER PARAMETERS: Adjusts rapidly to most water chemistries. Prefers a temperature of 75–82°F (24–28°C) but can tolerate temperatures well above or well below this range.

PROPAGATION: In the aquarium, cuttings from the rhizome. In terrariums, by seed. Successful seed production is rare in water.

NOTES: The naturally occurring *Anubias barteri* var. *nana* has long been used as a foreground plant. In some nano-tanks, it can also be used for midground planting. Generally grows 3–4 inches (8–10 cm) in height, though it can be taller. *A. barteri* var. *nana* is available in several color forms and leaf variations.

Anubias barteri var. *nana* "Petite"

The cultivar *Anubias barteri* var "Petite" is a wonderful, tiny plant ideally suited for foreground planting in nano-tanks. The leaves seldom exceed the diameter of a dime and height is rarely over 2 inches (5 cm). Plant in a group directly in the substrate or attach to small pieces of driftwood or rocks. Its diminutive size makes it easy to unintentionally bury the rhizome, so take care when planting.

The naturally occurring *A. barteri* "coffeefolia" is useful in larger nano-tanks of at least 10 gallons (38 L). It grows more rapidly than the other two forms and gets larger. Though typically 4–6 inches (10–15 cm) in height, it can exceed 12 inches (30 cm) in certain setups. Due to its size and rapid growth, it is best used as a single plant and can be a very eye-catching focal point.

Anubias barteri "Coffeefolia"

Cryptocoryne parva

CRYPTS *Cryptocoryne* species

OVERVIEW: *Cryptocoryne* may be the most diverse genus commonly kept by aquarists. It includes species that seldom reach 2 inches (5 cm) in height and those that can reach 6 feet, species whose leaves range from every shade of green imaginable to brown, pale red, and deep red. Sometimes there is one color on the top of the leaf and another color on the underside. Leaf shape can be short or long, narrow or broad, and is frequently cordate. The leaves can be smooth or bullate. Many species are suitable for nano-tanks. Correct identification of species can be difficult, as many are very similar and much of the literature is inaccurate. For the aquarist, it is more important to know how the plant grows submersed than the exact species ID.

HABITAT: Streams and marshy areas

NATIVE RANGE: Southeast Asia

LIGHTING: Crypts are more adaptable than their reputation might suggest and a great choice for low-light tanks. Most species can acclimate to high light.

WATER PARAMETERS: Most species prefer soft water with a mineral-rich substrate and a temperature of 73–80°F (23–27°C).

PROPAGATION: Most species spread via runners.

NOTES: Crypts are sensitive to changes in lighting and water conditions. They often experience *Cryptocoryne* "melt" or "rot" when they are moved to a new tank and sometimes when light bulbs are changed. When this happens, the leaves almost appear to melt before your eyes. Remove any affected leaves but don't panic, even if all the leaves die back. Most of all, don't pull the roots out. Leave them alone and the plants will usually recover.

Cryptocoryne becketii

Some of the best choices for nano-tanks are *C. parva*, the smallest crypt, *C. beckettii*, *C. "petchii,"* and *C. wendtii*. *C. wendtii* is available in many varieties, some naturally occurring and others produced in captivity. Green, brown, and red forms are all available. Examining the flower structure is the only way to differentiate many of the *Cryptocoryne* species.

Cryptocoryne wendtii "Broad Leaf"

BLACK AMAZON SWORDPLANT *Echinodorus parviflorus*
(Peruvian Swordplant)

OVERVIEW: The Black Amazon Sword is definitely the best choice among the traditional-looking swordplants for the nano-aquarium. Its growth form is very similar to species like *E. amazonicus* and *E. bleheri*, but it remains much smaller. This species is often referred to as *E. peruensis* in the aquarium literature. The Tropica or Rosetta Sword is a cultivar of this species that was developed at the Tropica Aquarium Plants nursery in Denmark.

HABITAT: This amphibious species grows in marshy areas.

NATIVE RANGE: Definite information is not known, but the native range is presumed to be Peru and Bolivia.

LIGHTING: Medium to bright

WATER PARAMETERS: Highly adaptable, soft or hard, 73–79°F (23–26°C)

PROPAGATION: *E. parviflorus* produces inflorescences (flowers) when grown in the aquarium. Adventitious plantlets form along the flower spike. When the adventitious plantlets have grown a few roots they can be cut off the spike and planted in the substrate.

NOTES: Black Amazon Swordplants are ideal as a mid-background focal point in most nano-aquascapes. Capable of growing up to approximately 10 inches (25 cm) in height, most specimens grow to about 8 inches (20 cm). Each plant can produce well over 30 leaves. Add some iron fertilizer to the substrate and don't bury the crown. This species is typically grown emersed commercially and will have to adapt to living in your aquarium. It will lose the outer row of leaves, possibly more. New growth will be softer and may vary a bit in color.

DWARF HAIRGRASS *Eleocharis* spp.
(Dwarf Spikerush, Spike Sedge)

OVERVIEW: Dwarf Hairgrasses are an excellent choice for creating a foreground carpet, as shown above in a 12-gallon shallow nano-tank. There are a number of very similar species that can confound even experts trying to assign proper IDs. Hairgrasses can be somewhat demanding, but the end result is worth the effort.

HABITAT: *Eleocharis* has some 250 species worldwide, from Amazon rainforest streams to the banks of rivers, ponds, and marshes in eastern North America. *Eleocharis parvula* is one common U.S. native that makes its way into the aquarium trade.

NATIVE RANGE: Worldwide.

LIGHTING: Medium to bright.

WATER PARAMETERS: pH 6–8, does well in soft to hard water, 68–74°F (20–23°C).

PROPAGATION: Via runners.

NOTES: Cool temperatures are the key to success with Dwarf Hairgrass. It's an ideal plant for tanks maintained in the low 70s°F (20s°C). High light is beneficial, as is the regular addition of iron fertilizer. Dosing with CO_2 is also appreciated. Plant small clumps 1–2 inches (2.5–5 cm) apart in the foreground, just deep enough to get them to stay planted. The stems are somewhat delicate, so soft, sandy substrates make it less likely that the aquarist will damage the stems when planting. In the right conditions they will spread and fill in to make very pleasing green mats. The tank above has a mix of *Eleocharis asicularis* and a *Lilaeopsis* species, another grassy, lawn-forming plant group known as micro-swords.

FINE LEAF ANACHARIS *Egeria najas*

OVERVIEW: Related to the venerable Anacharis, *Egeria densa, E. najas* is much more adaptable and an all-around better choice in most aquariums, but particularly in nano-tanks. This stem plant is capable of extremely rapid growth in ideal conditions and can be of great assistance in removing nutrients from the water column and thereby helping to eliminate algae blooms. Some hobbyists use rampant-growing plants such as this in new aquarium setups to help control spikes of ammonia, nitrite, and nitrate, which can be stressful or even fatal to fishes.

HABITAT: True aquatic species that typically grows in slow-moving stretches of rivers.

NATIVE RANGE: Brazil, Uruguay, Paraguay, and Argentina.

LIGHTING: Medium to bright.

WATER PARAMETERS: Highly adaptable to water chemistry. Does well in soft or moderately hard water, 70–76°F (21–24°C).

PROPAGATION: Cuttings from the central stem.

NOTES: Plant individual stems in the background with 0.75–1 inch between plants. Its beautiful shade of green and compact leaf formation make it an excellent backdrop to plants with different leaf shapes and colors. The stem may become brittle in hard water. The plant can be allowed to reach the surface before it is pruned. To prune, pinch the stems off just above one of the nodes to encourage branching of the plant.

Helanthium tenellum, the Pygmy Chain Sword

CHAIN SWORDPLANTS *Helanthium* species (formerly *Echinodorus* species)

OVERVIEW: The chain swordplants have long been considered to be members of the genus *Echinodorus*. Recent research indicates that they should be moved to the genus *Helanthium*, but much literature does yet not reflect this change. The various chain swords grow to different heights and differ from most *Echinodorus* in several ways. Most important to aquarists is that they reproduce by means of runners. These species can form dense mats. Due to the different heights reached by different species, they can be used in a number of locations in an aquascape. Growth is denser in higher light. *Echinodorus/Helanthium* are typically commercially cultured emersed, so they will need to acclimate to living submersed in the aquarium. At a minimum, the outer row of leaves will die back and sometimes all the existing leaves will die. The new leaves will be fleshier and have a slightly different shape. The leaves grow out of a crown or basal rosette. Be careful not to bury the crown in the substrate or the leaves may become damaged, which can ultimately result in the death of the plant. If the plant doesn't have enough roots to hold it down when you get it, you can very carefully plant it with the crown under the surface of the substrate. Go back in the tank approximately 10–14 days after planting and gently pull the plant up so that the crown is exposed. There should be sufficient new root growth by this point to anchor the plant. If the leaves turn yellowish, the plant is lacking iron. Plant in a substrate designed for plants or add laterite to the substrate. The regular addition of liquid iron fertilizer is also beneficial.

148

Helanthium bolivianum "latifolius"

HABITAT: Streamside or boggy/marshy areas that seasonally flood.
NATIVE RANGE: North to South America
LIGHTING: Medium to high
WATER PARAMETERS: pH 6–8.5, grows best in hard water but will adapt to soft water, 72–82°F (22–28°C).
PROPAGATION: By runners. Will flower and can also be propagated by seed.
NOTES: *H. tenellum*, the Pygmy Chain Swordplant, is the smallest species and typically grows about 2–3 inches (5–8 cm) in height. This is an ideal foreground plant. The correct identification of the chain sword *H. latifolium* is up for debate. It may turn out to be *H. bolivianum* or a different growth form of *H. tenellum*. This form typically grows 3–4 inches (8–10 cm) in height and has narrow leaves.

Another fast-spreading and easy-to-keep pygmy chain sword is *Helanthium bolivianum* "Angustifolious." In strong light, paradoxically, it will stay shorter and more compact; otherwise it becomes tall and is best used as a background plant. Needs periodic trimming.

Helanthium bolivianum "Angustifolius"

PEARLWEED *Hemianthus micranthemoides*

OVERVIEW: *Hemianthus micranthemoides* is a beautiful, relatively undemanding stem plant that can be used quite effectively to carpet the foreground of a nano-tank. In very shallow tanks, it can be used as a midground plant.

HABITAT: Pearlweed grows along river banks, where it can be either submersed or emersed, depending on time of year and rainfall.

NATIVE RANGE: Southeastern United States

LIGHTING: Medium to bright

WATER PARAMETERS: Highly adaptable to varying water chemistry. Does well in soft or hard water, 74–79°F (23–26°C).

PROPAGATION: Cuttings from the central stem

NOTES: Plant individual stems in the foreground with 0.5–1 inch (1.3–2.5 cm) between plants. It can be laid down horizontally rather than planted vertically. If this is done, new shoots will emerge from the nodes along the stem, giving a more lush growth. It will sometimes grow over driftwood or rocks if planted horizontally, which is aesthetically very appealing. Leaves will form more densely in brighter light. Pinch the stems off just above one of the nodes when they reach 3–4 inches (7.6–10 cm) in height to encourage bushier growth and prevent the loss of the lower leaves.

CORKSCREW VALLISNERIA *Vallisneria tortifolia*

OVERVIEW: This venerable aquarium plant has been a favorite of aquarists for a very long time. The name *V. tortifolia* is not valid but is rather a trade name. This species has been in the hobby so long that much of the original information about it has been forgotten. It is probably one of the growth forms of *V. americana* but that is difficult to verify. By the same token, there does not seem to be any reliable information on where this plant grows in the wild. We do know that it is a true aquatic and how to care for it in the aquarium.

LIGHTING: Medium to bright.

WATER PARAMETERS: 6.5-8.5, moderately hard to hard, 72-82 F

PROPAGATION: Propagation is via runners.

NOTES: Corkscrew Vallisneria typically grows to somewhere around 6-8" in height making it well suited for mid-ground planting in most nano aquaria. It propagates rapidly via runners and can form somewhat tall carpets over time. The corkscrewing of the leaves is very interesting and contrasts nicely with more typically shaped leaves of other species in the aquascape. The leaves are soft enough to sway in the current, adding to its appeal. Growth will be more vigorous when iron fertilizers are added regularly.

STREAM BOGMOSS *Mayaca fluviatilis*
(Bogmoss)

OVERVIEW: One of the more demanding plants included in this volume, *M. fluviatilis* is well worth a little extra effort. This stem plant produces beautiful, fine, light green leaves that make a beautiful background for darker green or red plants.

HABITAT: The species name *fluviatilis*—meaning "in or near rivers"—accurately describes this plant's habitat. This species generally grows in rivers and sometimes emersed along the bank.

NATIVE RANGE: Southern US south into Brazil

LIGHTING: Medium to bright

WATER PARAMETERS: pH 5–7.5, soft to moderate, 70–78°F (21–26°C)

PROPAGATION: *M. fluviatilis* is most commonly propagated by cuttings from the stem. In ideal conditions, it can produce lateral shoots.

NOTES: Laterite should be added to the substrate, and the regular addition of liquid fertilizers containing iron is a necessity. The stems of Stream Bogmoss are delicate, so care must be taken when planting them. As a consequence, a soft, sandy substrate is preferred. Plant two or three stems together and plant the groups about 1 inch (2.5 cm) apart to allow enough light to reach the lower leaves so that they do not drop off. This species appreciates some water movement and its beauty is enhanced as it sways in the current. The addition of CO_2 is beneficial but not required.

JAVA FERN *Microsorum pteropus*

OVERVIEW: Java Fern is a classic aquarium plant, widely favored by aquarists for its ability to survive in dim lighting and its apparently bad-tasting leaves, which allow it to be kept successfully with a number of herbivorous fish species. A number of variants with distinctive leaf shapes and sizes are now available.

HABITAT: This is an amphibious species that grows in water or in humid forest habitats.

NATIVE RANGE: Southeast Asia

LIGHTING: Does best in low lighting but will also thrive in medium lighting.

WATER PARAMETERS: pH 6–7.5, soft to moderate, 70–80°F (21–27°C)

PROPAGATION: Propagation is via cuttings from the rhizome or the formation of adventitious plantlets at the tips of older leaves and sometimes at the bases of leaves.

NOTES: Java Ferns grow on creeping rhizomes. Attach the rhizomes to driftwood or rocks by tying them loosely with nylon fishing line or similar material. The rhizomes should never be buried in the substrate. In the typical form, the leaves can be up to 3 inches (7.6 cm) wide at the base and may exceed 30 inches (76 cm) in length. Fortunately, they seldom reach this size and doing so takes years. Typical growth is much smaller, with most energy devoted to growing horizontally rather than vertically. Still, using this form in nano-tanks requires occasionally removing larger specimens and letting the adventitious plants grow up to take their place. Leaves turning black may indicate a need to feed the plant.

DWARF RED THAI LILY *Nymphaea rubra*

OVERVIEW: This true water lily doesn't grow as large as the more commonly kept night-blooming tropical lilies. In the aquarium, if the plants are not allowed to form floating pads they become spectacular foreground to midground focal points for nano-tanks, producing 30–50 leaves. If they are able to form floating pads, they provide great shelter for many fishes and potential spawning sites for labyrinth fishes. Similar species are *N. stellata* (green leaves) and *N. micrantha* (green with brown mottling).

HABITAT: Still or slow-flowing waterways

NATIVE RANGE: *Nymphaea rubra* and *N. stellata*: Southeast Asia. *N. micrantha*: West Africa

LIGHTING: Will thrive under almost any lighting, including dim.

WATER PARAMETERS: pH 6–8, moderate to hard, 70–80°F (21–27°C)

PROPAGATION: Grows from a bulb and produces runners.

NOTES: Lest it take over a nano tank, pinch the floating leaves (those with long stems and floating leaves) off at their bases before they reach the surface. Do this diligently and they will eventually stop forming floating pads. These species all benefit from iron-rich substrates. Drop the bulb into position but not do not bury it in the substrate. It will put out roots and attach itself. Water lily fertilizer tabs can be added to the substrate directly under the plant but will encourage the formation of more surface pads and flowers, do not use them if submersed growth is desired. The plant will sometimes go seasonally dormant and drop most of its leaves.

SLENDER PONDWEED *Potamogeton gayi*
(Triangle Pondweed)

OVERVIEW: This is an easily maintained, unusually shaped, true aquatic species. Slender Pondweed's overall shape is somewhat reminiscent of a corn plant, but on a much smaller scale. It is a South American native and one of approximately 100 *Potamogeton* species known throughout the world. it can be very useful for creating a South American biotope and grows quickly once established.

HABITAT: Ponds and lakes

NATIVE RANGE: Southern South America

LIGHTING: Medium to bright

WATER PARAMETERS: pH 6–7.5, soft to moderate, 70–78°F (21–26°C)

PROPAGATION: *P. gayi* can be propagated by cuttings from the central stem. It also regularly produces runners.

NOTES: Extremely adaptable and relatively slender, this species is a good choice for the background of any small aquarium. Narrow leaves offer a nice textural contrast in most aquascapes. Beware of fishes that might nibble plants; the soft leaves of *P. gayi* may prove too tempting for them. Plant individually in clusters with enough space between the plants so that you don't damage them when planting the next one. They seem more likely to produce runners in hard water and when receiving regular additions of iron fertilizer. If a plant gets too tall, cut the stem just above one of the nodes.

CRYSTALWORT *Riccia fluitans*

OVERVIEW: In the old days, this plant was considered a very easy species to grow in moderate light and somewhat hard water. Today, it is considered a difficult plant to grow, requiring very high light and soft water. In the past, this species was allowed to grow naturally, so the tiny individual plants would form clumps that floated at or just below the surface of the water. As part of the "nature aquarium" revolution, hobbyists began trying to force this species to grow attached to rocks or driftwood to simulate terrestrial bushes, a much more involved undertaking.

HABITAT: Still or slow-flowing waters, sometimes found growing on the bank during low-water season.

NATIVE RANGE: Worldwide

LIGHTING: Medium to high

WATER PARAMETERS: pH 6–8.5, soft to hard, 70–78°F (21–26°C)

PROPAGATION: Tiny individual plants form large colonies. Taking some of the individual plants and adding them to another tank or tying them to a substrate is all that is required for propagation.

NOTES: Very easy to grow as a floating plant. Success with submersed culture requires tying a clump of *R. fluitans* to a piece of rock or driftwood with nylon fishing line or some similar material and growing it under intense lighting, preferably with CO_2 injection, until the desired look is achieved. Then it can be placed in the display tank. Of course, it will not continue to grow this way, so a number of clumps must be under cultivation so a new one can be moved into the display tank when the original one starts to lose its shape and condition.

PINK ROTALA *Rotala rotundifolia*
(Dwarf Rotala)

OVERVIEW: *Rotala rotundifolia* is the easiest-to-grow member of a very beautiful genus. It grows well in almost any water chemistry and under all but the dimmest light. The only difference when conditions are less than ideal is the color of the leaves. The happier the plant, the brighter the pink on the leaves will be. Older leaves near the base of the stem tend to be green. but new growth should be pink to red. Brighter light, feeding, and supplementing with CO_2 will help bring the plant into its full splendor.

HABITAT: Pink Rotala is a creeping marsh plant.

NATIVE RANGE: Widespread in Southeast Asia, ranging from India to Japan

LIGHTING: Medium to bright

WATER PARAMETERS: pH 6-8, soft to hard, 72-82°F (22-28°C)

PROPAGATION: Propagation is easy: Snip cuttings from the central stem. Plant in substrate. Regular pruning will yield new plants and encourage the mother plants to become bushier.

NOTES: Some aquarists report that their best successes with Pink Rotala have been in relatively hard, alkaline water with temperatures in the mid-70s°F (20s°C) and the regular addition of iron fertilizer. Plant two or three stems together and leave approximately 1-1.5 inches (2.5-4 cm) between sets. It is best used as a background plant with darker green plants in front of it.

DWARF SAGITTARIA *Sagittaria subulata* var. *pusilla*

OVERVIEW: This is the smallest form of *Sagittaria*. It is an excellent choice for creating foreground carpets in soft water aquariums.

HABITAT: A marginal species that grows along slow-moving stretches of rivers and in marshes

NATIVE RANGE: Southeastern United States

LIGHTING: Medium to bright

WATER PARAMETERS: Somewhat adaptable to water chemistry, soft, 70-76°F (21-24°C)

PROPAGATION: Via runners

NOTES: Plant individual stems in the foreground with 0.5-1 inches (1.3-2.5 cm) between plants. Dwarf Sag will spread rapidly and will fill in the open space in a short time. A plant substrate or the addition of iron to fine gravel will help it become established and spread more quickly. Height is variable but is typically 1-2 inches (2.5-5 cm). *Sagittaria* and *Vallisneria* generally don't do well together. The genus that the water conditions favor (soft for *Sagittaria* or hard for *Vallisneria*) will outcompete the other and eventually take over the tank.

JAVA MOSS *Vesicularia dubyana*

OVERVIEW: One of the easiest aquarium plants to grow. A big clump of Java Moss provides a wonderful habitat for a thriving microfauna culture, which in turn provides a ready source of food for tiny fry and even for the adults of small species. Many egg-scattering fishes will use *V. dubyana* as a spawning medium, and small shrimp like to hide in it.

HABITAT: *V. dubyana* covers fallen trees, rock, or soil in moist jungle areas and is more likely to be found out of water than in it.

NATIVE RANGE: Southeast Asia

LIGHTING: Low to medium

WATER PARAMETERS: pH 6–7.5, soft to moderate, 70–78°F (21–26°C)

PROPAGATION: If left alone, forms a ball-like clump attached to a hard substrate. Propagation is simply a matter of pulling a handful off the clump.

NOTES: Grows well in almost any aquarium, including low light tanks. A little bit goes a long way when Java Moss is attached to a piece of driftwood or a rock in a nano-tank. Keep it trimmed or it will take over the entire aquascape.

Greatly enlarged portrait of a Green Shrimp in a planted nano-aquarium.

A new world of spineless wonders

Among the most exciting developments in freshwater aquarium-keeping is the growing availability of invertebrate animals, many of them ideally suited for life in a nano-ecosystem. Where generations of aquarists in the past had few invertebrate choices, we now have ready access to a world of ornamental shrimp, micro-crabs, very colorful crayfishes, and snails that are prized for their beauty and not just their grazing talents.

Before simply adding any of the following nano-invertebrates to your system, a few basic background facts are worth knowing. The first has to do with pairing ornamental crustaceans with fishes in a tank: unless the fishes are specialized algae-grazers, if they can eat a shrimp or baby shrimp, they absolutely will. Many of the fish species profiled in these pages have proven to be most suitable for a community tank that includes small invertebrates. But invertebrates are not nearly as flexible as fishes when it comes to water conditions. They will not tolerate any detectable amount of nitrite or ammonia, and only the lowest level of nitrate. Because of this, they need an aquarium that is well cycled and established and a diligent caretaker to maintain it. Many species are also extremely particular about water temperature and hardness, and it is important to research their needs in order to have success.

With invertebrates, stocking density protocol is very different as well. Many more invertebrates than fishes can be housed in a relatively small volume. Hundreds of shrimp can be kept together comfortably, as they are completely peaceful. Attention must be paid to water filtration and oxygenation when keeping any delicate crustaceans. Shrimp-specific tanks that are planted and established need to be fed only a few times a week. Shrimp graze constantly and rarely need large meals.

The popularity of snails, too, is skyrocketing as nano-aquariums attract new enthusiasts. Many snails, including the vast array of *Neritina* and *Clithon* species, are exceptional algae-eaters. Care must be taken not to stock them too densely: keeping one snail per 5 gallons of tank space is recommended, as they can easily starve once the available algae has been depleted.

CRYSTAL RED SHRIMP *Caridina* cf. *cantonensis*
(CRS, Red Crystal Bee)

OVERVIEW: This dwarf species is one of the most popular because of its vibrant coloration and striking patterning. While more particular about water temperature and pH, it will breed easily given the proper conditions. There is a lot of variety to the patterning available, and the shrimp are graded based on quality of color and striping. These do not hybridize with the genus *Neocaridina* and the two can be housed together safely. Like all shrimp, they are very sensitive to water quality, so overfeeding should be avoided. A few small meals per week are generally adequate.

NATIVE RANGE: Southern China for wild types; domestically bred color forms

MAXIMUM SIZE: 1.2 in. (3 cm)

MINIMUM AQUARIUM SIZE: 2 gal. (8 L)

WATER REQUIREMENTS: pH 6–7.5, 65–75°F (18–24°C).

FEEDING: Omnivorous and herbivorous. Feed algae-based pellets or flake, and offer high-protein foods sparingly. Be careful not to overfeed.

BEHAVIOR & CARE: Slightly more challenging than *Neocaridina*, *Caridina cantonensis* comes in a wide range of patterns and colors. Most popular and readily available are the Crystal Red and Crystal Black, which are line-bred forms of the wild bee. Wild bees come in a range of colors, including tan and white, red and white, black and white, and blue and white. The selectively bred species require soft, cooler water and will produce offspring with varying patterns. Selective breeding must be maintained for consistent color patterns.

Like fancy Koi, Crystal Red Shrimp are the result of intensive breeding efforts.

These shrimp do best in groups of at least five or six adults, and they enjoy a planted aquarium. For best breeding results, they should not be paired with fishes except with caution. Most adult shrimp can cohabitate with dwarf species of fishes that do not get larger than one inch.

The most suitable species are those from the *Boraras* genus, some *Breviboras*, and *Trigonostigma*, as well as some specialized grazers like *Otocinclus*, *Parotocinclus*, and even some *Stiphodon* species. One should avoid pairing them with fishes that are micro-predators, like danios and most tetras, as they will readily predate upon young shrimp.

Wild-type female Caridina cantonensis *"Bee".*

TIGER SHRIMP *Caridina* cf. *cantonensis* "Tiger"
(Super Tiger)

OVERVIEW: Tiger Shrimp are one of the more popular shrimps in the hobby. They reproduce readily in the correct conditions, and can be a striking addition to a small planted tank. Start with at least five or six shrimp as a foundation breeding colony.

NATIVE RANGE: Southern China

MAXIMUM SIZE: 1.4 in. (3.5 cm)

MINIMUM AQUARIUM SIZE: 2 gal. (8 L)

WATER PARAMETERS: pH 6.5–7.5, 65–75°F (18–24°C)

FEEDING: Omnivorous. Be cautious and do not overfeed; like other shrimp species, they are highly sensitive to poor water quality. A good herbivorous pellet or flake should be fed sparingly, no more than a few times a week.

BEHAVIOR & CARE: There are two main color variations of the wild Tiger Shrimp. The first is grey with dark brown stripes, the second bluish with dark brown stripes. They may have a golden to orange head and tail, and sometimes have white or tan striping behind the dark stripes. Occasionally one comes across one that has red stripes as well, though this is less common. (The two specimens at right were produced by a German aquarium breeder.) Several mutations have become very popular in the hobby, one of which is a dark blue color. There are also "blondes," which have light gold eyes. Hybridization between these and bee shrimp is very prevalent, so care should be taken not to house them with others of this genus and species type.

BLUE TIGER SHRIMP *Caridina* cf. *cantonensis* "Tiger"
(Super Tiger)
NATIVE RANGE: Southern China (captive bred)
MAXIMUM SIZE: 1.4 in. (3.5 cm)
MINIMUM AQUARIUM SIZE: 2 gal. (8 L)

TANGERINE TIGER SHRIMP *Caridina serrata*
(Orange Tupfel)
NATIVE RANGE: Southern China
MAXIMUM SIZE: 1.4 in. (3.5 cm)
MINIMUM AQUARIUM SIZE: 2 gal. (8 L)

GREEN SHRIMP *Caridina* cf. *babaulti* var. Green
(Horseradish Shrimp, Rainbow Shrimp)

OVERVIEW: Green Shrimp are true gems in the invertebrate world and do not hybridize with most of the other commonly available species. They have a more serrated rostrum, or nose, and are often called Rainbow Shrimp because they can change color subtly based on water parameters. They are very sensitive to water quality, so a clean, established, and well-oxygenated tank is an absolute must. Be sure to have adequate and well-maintained filtration in place.

NATIVE RANGE: India, Malaysia

MAXIMUM SIZE: 1.2 in. (3 cm)

MINIMUM AQUARIUM SIZE: 2 gal. (8 L)

WATER PARAMETERS: pH 6.5–7.5, 65–75°F (18–24°C)

FEEDING: Omnivorous. Offer a good quality pellet or flake high in algae and low in protein. Gel foods for shrimp, such as "Shrimp Souffle," are an excellent choice.

BEHAVIOR & CARE: Highly variable in color forms, these can range in hue from a transparent tan through black, dark blue, and neon yellow to a deep, dark green. They are a hardy shrimp once established, and won't hybridize with the Asian species of *Caridina* (CRS, Tiger, etc.) or *Neocaridina*. Often fragile upon import, once established they make a huge impact in a planted or invertebrate tank with their striking colors. Care should be taken not to house them with fishes larger than 1 inch (2.5 cm) or those with a strong prey drive, like dwarf cichlids.

AMANO SHRIMP *Caridina multidentata*
(Yamato Shrimp, Japonica Shrimp, Algae Shrimp)

OVERVIEW: The Amano Shrimp, which readily eats filamentous algae, is truly the workhorse of dwarf shrimps and the most popular addition to a planted tank. They are low-order breeders, so they do not reproduce in fresh water but have a relatively long life span and large size, making them popular in most community tanks. Stock at a rate of up to 10 shrimp per gallon (3.8 L) of water.

NATIVE RANGE: Taiwan, Japan

MAXIMUM SIZE: 2 in. (3 cm)

MINIMUM AQUARIUM SIZE: 2 gal. (8 L)

WATER PARAMETERS: pH 6.2–8, 70–84°F (21–29°C)

FEEDING: Omnivorous. Amano Shrimp will readily eat most algae and are easy to supplement with prepared foods like pellets or flake. If you want them to eat algae, feed supplemental foods sparingly. Avoid food too high in protein.

BEHAVIOR & CARE: The Amano Shrimp is one of the largest of the dwarf shrimps and can take a wide range of temperatures. Because of their size, they can outcompete smaller shrimp for food, so care should be taken with stocking density in a small tank. Due to their large size, they are an appropriate component of a mix that includes most community type fishes. Many people keep them in discus tanks, as they are tolerant of the higher temperatures and are efficient at cleaning up uneaten foods. Fishes like angels should be avoided, though larger tetras, danios, and most *Corydoras* catfishes, as well as *Ancistrus* and *Hypancistrus*, are appropriate.

167

BUMBLEBEE SHRIMP *Caridina breviata*

OVERVIEW: This wild shrimp looks very similar to the Bee Shrimp, *Caridina cantonensis*, but differs in that it almost always has a dark head and generally wide striping ranging from black to brown, with beige or colorless contrasting stripes. Maximum stocking density should be about 10 adult shrimp per gallon (38 L).

NATIVE RANGE: Southern China, captive-bred

MAXIMUM SIZE: 1.2 in. (3 cm)

MINIMUM AQUARIUM SIZE: 2 gal. (8 L)

WATER PARAMETERS: pH 6–7.5, 65–75°F (18–24°C)

FEEDING: Omnivorous. Avoid high protein; a range of herbivorous pellets or flakes is appropriate.

BEHAVIOR & CARE: With the right conditions, this is a relatively hardy shrimp. Make sure to keep its tank cool and well oxygenated. Be cautious of overfeeding, as changes in tank chemistry can be lethal to shrimp. This shrimp can be housed with species of *Neocaridina* or peaceful fishes 1 inch (2.5 cm) and under. One should avoid housing them with larger, more active fishes, as their young are easy prey. They should not be housed with other species of Asian *Caridina* (CRS, Tiger, etc.) because there is a strong risk of hybridization.

RED BUMBLEBEE SHRIMP *Caridina breviata*
NATIVE RANGE: Southern China, captive-bred
MAXIMUM SIZE: 1.2 in. (3 cm)
MINIMUM AQUARIUM SIZE: 2 gal. (8 L)

BUMBLEBEE SHRIMP *Caridina breviata*
NATIVE RANGE: Southern China, captive-bred
MAXIMUM SIZE: 1.2 in. (3 cm)
MINIMUM AQUARIUM SIZE: 2 gal. (8 L)

MALAWA SHRIMP *Caridina pareparensis parvidentata*

OVERVIEW: A small species from Sulawesi, this shrimp is known for its rapid reproduction. They are not brightly colored, but extremely durable and easy to raise, and they do not hybridize with any other species commonly sold in the hobby. Start a breeding colony with a minimum of five or six shrimp. Maximum stocking density should be about 10 adult shrimp per gallon (38 L).

NATIVE RANGE: Sulawesi

MAXIMUM SIZE: 1 in. (2.5 cm)

MINIMUM AQUARIUM SIZE: 2 gal. (8 L)

WATER PARAMETERS: pH 7–8.5, 68–86°F (20-30°C)

FEEDING: Omnivorous. Pellets and flakes are readily accepted.

BEHAVIOR & CARE: Because of their extremely fast reproduction, they can often outcompete other species of shrimp for food and can become the dominant species. It is important to make sure there is ample space for the population to increase, despite their small size. While not as flashy as many other shrimp, they are an excellent choice for a beginner or as an addition to a small invertebrate tank. Their small size makes them less than ideal to combine with most fishes, though species like *Boraras* or snails are a good choice. If your shrimp are breeding successfully, you will need to harvest some periodically, and there should be no shortage of people willing to buy them or barter for other species.

SUNKIST SHRIMP *Caridina thambipillai*
(*Caridina propinqua*, Orange Shrimp)

OVERVIEW: Commonly found in the pet trade, Sunkist Shrimp are a striking addition to a small planted tank. They are low-order breeders, meaning there is a larval stage for the young, but hobbyists have succeeded in breeding them.

NATIVE RANGE: Indonesia

MAXIMUM SIZE: 1.2 in. (3 cm)

MINIMUM AQUARIUM SIZE: 2 gal. (8 L)

WATER PARAMETERS: pH 6–8, 75–85°F (24–29°C)

FEEDING: Omnivorous. Feed a balanced diet of pelleted or flake foods, avoiding very high protein.

BEHAVIOR & CARE: This species is a great addition to a planted invertebrate tank, as they won't hybridize with the other *Neocaridina* or *Caridina* species commonly found in the hobby. They are brightly colored, peaceful, and easy to keep. A brown version is also available. As with all shrimp, care should be taken with tankmates to prevent predation. Small, peaceful species of danios, tetras, microrasboras, and *Boraras*, as well as small catfishes or loaches from the *Petruichthys* or *Micronemacheilus* families, are acceptable. Start a breeding colony with a minimum of five or six shrimp. Maximum stocking density should be about 10 adult shrimp per gallon (38 L).

RED CHERRY SHRIMP *Neocaridina davidi*
(Cherry Shrimp, Red Cherry, Red Fire)

OVERVIEW: One of the most common and popular freshwater dwarf shrimps, Red Cherry is an excellent choice for the beginning shrimp-keeper. They are relatively durable and accepting of a range of water chemistries, and a striking addition to a small tank. Cherry Shrimp breed readily with good care; the young hatch into miniature versions of the adults.

NATIVE RANGE: Taiwan, cultivated in pet trade

MAXIMUM SIZE: 1.2 in. (3 cm), females slightly larger than males

MINIMUM AQUARIUM SIZE: 2 gal. (8 L)

WATER PARAMETERS: pH 6–8, 60–82°F (16–28°C)

FEEDING: Omnivorous and herbivorous. Feed algae-based pellets and flake; feed high-protein foods sparingly.

BEHAVIOR & CARE: Cherry Shrimp are extremely peaceful, totally plant-safe, and easy to feed. They will accept a range of foods from pelleted to flake to live, though care must be taken not to overfeed. Offering a small amount of food a few times a week is usually adequate. Excess food should be removed to prevent fouling of the water. Shrimp are best kept in small groups; 10 or more are recommended. Good tankmates include Nerite snails, algae-eaters like *Otocinclus*, and small schooling fishes like *Boraras brigittae* (Chili Rasbora). Fishes with a strong prey drive (barbs, large danios, and large tetras) should be avoided. For the best success in breeding, an invertebrate-only tank is preferred. Several variants of the species have been bred, including the Sakura, Painted Fire Red, Yellow Fire, Orange, Chocolate, and Rili (in various colors).

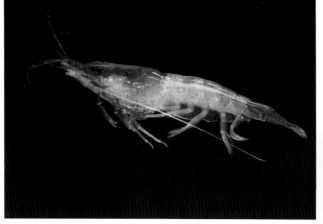

RED RILI SHRIMP *Neocaridina davidi* var. "Red Rili"
NATIVE RANGE: Taiwan, cultivated in pet trade
MAXIMUM SIZE: 1.2 in. (3 cm), females slightly larger than males
MINIMUM AQUARIUM SIZE: 2 gal. (8 L)

YELLOW SHRIMP *Neocaridina davidi* var. "Yellow"
NATIVE RANGE: Taiwan, cultivated in pet trade
MAXIMUM SIZE: 1.2 in. (3 cm), females slightly larger than males
MINIMUM AQUARIUM SIZE: 2 gal. (8 L)

SNOWBALL SHRIMP *Neocaridina palmata*
(White Pearl, Blue Pearl, Marbled, Rainbow, Blueberry Shrimp, Blackberry Shrimp)

OVERVIEW: These shrimp are easy to keep and peaceful toward other livestock. A planted tank with clean, oxygen-rich water is a perfect choice for this family of shrimp. Start a breeding colony with a minimum of five or six. Maximum stocking density should be about 10 adults per gallon (3.8 L). The specimen shown is a captive-bred Snowball carrying eggs; it is sometimes called the White Pearl Shrimp.

NATIVE RANGE: Southern China; domestic sources

MAXIMUM SIZE: 1.2 in. (3 cm)

WATER PARAMETERS: pH 6.5–8, 60–82°F (16–28°C)

MINIMUM AQUARIUM SIZE: 2 gal. (8 L)

FEEDING: Omnivorous and herbivorous; algae-based pelleted foods or flake, high-protein foods

BEHAVIOR & CARE: The wild form of this shrimp can range in color from blue to black to tan, with some speckling and striping. They have been domestically selectively bred in order to produce white and blue strains, as well as others. These shrimp are very hardy, but should not be kept with other *Neocaridina* species, as hybridization is likely. As your shrimp population grows, you will need to harvest some periodically, and there should be no shortage of people willing to buy them or barter for other species. If you see especially interesting color forms, segregate them into their own tank or remove all others and attempt to breed a line with your own distinctive color form.

GREEN LACE SHRIMP *Atyoida pilipes*
(Sulawesi Fan Shrimp)

OVERVIEW: The Green Lace Shrimp is one of the smallest fan filter-feeding shrimps available. Because their fans are relatively short and bristly, they are among the easiest to maintain in a freshwater aquarium. Stock in groups of at least five or six to establish a breeding population.

NATIVE RANGE: Indonesia, New Guinea, Philippines

MAXIMUM SIZE: 2.4 in. (6 cm)

MINIMUM AQUARIUM SIZE: 10 gal. (38 L), must be mature

WATER PARAMETERS: pH 6.5–8, 72–80°F (22–27°C)

FEEDING: Fan filter-feeder. Small crushed foods are required. Microcrustaceans like *Daphnia* or crushed flake work well.

BEHAVIOR & CARE: Green Lace Shrimp are entirely peaceful and a welcome addition to a hillstream or peaceful community tank. While they do not require current, it aids them in using their fans to remove particulates from the water column. (Nano-scale powerhead pumps are available and affordable at any good aquarium retail store.) Unlike larger fan filters, theirs are functional and can be used to pick up fine foods as a normal part of feeding. An established tank is a necessity for any of these filtering species, and species that are aggressive should be avoided. Many enjoy keeping these in tanks with strong directional flow and high oxygenation paired with species like *Stiphodons*, *Sewellia* sp. hillsteam loaches, and fast-moving danios.

DWARF ORANGE CRAYFISH *Cambarellus patzcuarensis* sp. "Orange"
(Mexican Dwarf Orange Crayfish, CPO)

OVERVIEW: At just over 1 inch, this small crayfish is an excellent addition to a planted invertebrate tank. They are plant-, fish-, shrimp-, and snail-safe and, like the dwarf shrimps, breed readily. Very sassy in nature, they add bright color and tons of personality to tanks of all sizes. They can be aggressive toward each other during breeding, so careful attention should be paid to stocking density and tank size as their numbers increase from breeding.

NATIVE RANGE: Lake Patzcuaro, Mexico, domestically bred

MAXIMUM SIZE: 1.25 in. (3.2 cm)

MINIMUM AQUARIUM SIZE: 5 gal. (19 L)

WATER PARAMETERS: pH 7–8, 70–78°F (21–26°C)

FEEDING: The CPO readily accepts most dried or pelleted foods, but should be offered a diet consisting of a good mix of meaty and herbivorous foods, with carotenoids for color. Care should be taken not to overfeed, as they are sensitive to water quality like most invertebrates.

BEHAVIOR & CARE: They are peaceful, but care should be taken to provide ample hiding spaces for crayfishes so they can avoid each other and prevent damage after molting. Stacked driftwood, ceramic, clay or PVC caves, or areas of dense planting are good options. They do well in an invertebrate tank or paired with most small, peaceful community fishes. As with other dwarf species, nippy or prey-driven fishes like dwarf cichlids should be avoided, as they will predate upon young crayfishes.

MICRO CRAB *Limnopilos naiyanetri*
(Thai Crab, Spider Crab)

OVERVIEW: One of the smallest fully aquatic freshwater crabs, the Micro Crab is a wonderful addition to an invertebrate tank. They are safe with dwarf shrimps and snails, and can be housed with small fishes. They are largely nocturnal and tend to collect in surface plants or areas of dense growth.

NATIVE RANGE: Thailand

MAXIMUM SIZE: 0.4 in. (1 cm)

MINIMUM AQUARIUM SIZE: 1 gal. (4 L)

WATER PARAMETERS: pH 6.5–8, 70–82°F (21–28°C)

FEEDING: They use setae, or bristles, on their claws to collect fine foods, so ground flake, soft pellets, or frozen microcrustaceans make up a suitable diet.

BEHAVIOR & CARE: These crabs are fully aquatic, needing no landing to exit the water, and are believed to complete their life cycle in fresh water. The female carries eggs, which turn from orange to yellow to gray, under her apron. They hatch into zoae and are supposed to hatch in full fresh water. There are few confirmed reports of successfully rearing the young in captivity, at least none with documentation. New breeding reports suggest the young are held until postlarval conversion is complete. Based on anecdotal evidence, it is thought that a light is necessary to help the larvae orient. These crabs are largely nocturnal and a bit shy. Care should be taken when selecting tankmates to ensure that the crabs are not picked on. Small fishes like *Boraras*, *Microdevario*, or *Trigonostigma* species are great choices, as are other invertebrates like dwarf shrimp and snails.

ASSASSIN SNAIL *Clea helena*
(*Anentome helena*)

OVERVIEW: The Assassin Snail has become increasingly popular since its introduction to the hobby. It readily eats Malaysian Trumpet Snails, pond snails, and bladder snails, and will also attack other ornamental snails. It is slower to breed than the pest snails, so it can be a good solution to pest snail problems.

NATIVE RANGE: Malaysia, Indonesia

MAXIMUM SIZE: 1 in. (2.5 cm)

MINIMUM AQUARIUM SIZE: 1 gal. (4 L)

WATER PARAMETERS: pH 7–8.5, 70–78°F (21–26°C); 72–74°F (22–23°C) is optimal,

FEEDING: Assassins will eat any ornamental or pest snails but are easily supplemented with frozen bloodworms or meaty pellets.

BEHAVIOR & CARE: The Assassin Snail is unassuming in its care, requiring a food source and little else. It is compatible with all community species except for other snails. There are reports of Assassins predating upon weakened shrimp and fishes, though this is uncommon. They lay single eggs along the bases of firm plant structures (like *Anubias*) or within hardscape, including driftwood, decorations, and sponge filtration. The eggs are laid singly, though prolifically, and are slow-growing, often taking a few months to become easy to see. Care should be taken to ensure that plants shared with other hobbyists do not contain the eggs, unless specified as such.

MYSTERY SNAIL *Pomacea bridgesii diffusa*
(Mystery Apple Snail, Spike-Topped Apple Snail)

OVERVIEW: Available in a wide range of colors and often having a vivid striped pattern, these snails are sexually specific, allowing controlled reproduction. Mystery Snails are a colorful and energetic addition to a small tank. They are peaceful and attractive, so they are a good foil for most invertebrates or community fishes.

NATIVE RANGE: Amazon basin, introduced invasively to SE Asia

MAXIMUM SIZE: 2 in. (5 cm)

MINIMUM AQUARIUM SIZE: 2.5 gal. (9 L)

WATER PARAMETERS: pH 7–8.5, 70–78°F (21–26°C); 72–74°F (22–23°C) is optimal.

FEEDING: While these snails are easy to feed, it is important to provide a calcium-rich diet to ensure healthy shell growth. Blanched vegetables or a calcium-enriched gelatinized food are ideal.

BEHAVIOR & CARE: Mystery Snails lay their eggs outside of the water line, in large clutches that are pink and resemble clusters of grapes. Because of this, it is important to allow a few inches of space on the glass for them to lay their clutches, or they will venture outside the tank to do so. Soft water will erode their shells and make them prone to fractures, which can be life threatening. Hard, cool water is best for their longevity. They are plant-safe and do well with other invertebrates or peaceful community fishes like mid-sized tetras, danios, and catfishes. They are a very poor pairing with any cichlid or larger tetra, which may mistake their antennae for worms.

NERITE SNAILS *Neritina* spp.

(Zebra, Horned, Bumblebee, Tracked, Red Spot, Tiger, Batik, Mini, Baseball Cap, Olive)

OVERVIEW: Nerite snails have become increasingly popular with freshwater aquarists because of their amazing ability to eat algae. Because their antennae and vulnerable face parts are barely visible, they can even be housed with some African Cichlids. They are excellent at helping to maintain rocks and hardscape, and are plant, fish, and invertebrate-safe. There are many species available in the pet trade. A Batik Nerite is shown above with small Bumblebee Nerites.

NATIVE RANGE: A broad distribution; most in the pet trade originate in Southeast Asia, though there are different types from all over the world, including the United States.

MAXIMUM SIZE: Varies by species, but generally less than 1.5 in. (4 cm) in diameter

MINIMUM AQUARIUM SIZE: Due to dietary needs, 5 gal. (19 L) is recommended.

WATER PARAMETERS: pH 7–8, 65–85°F (18–29°C)

FEEDING: Obligate algae grazers, Nerite snails eat all soft, flat types of algae. They are difficult to supplement, so care should be taken to give them ample space to graze on algae and infusoria. An established tank with stable water parameters is preferred.

BEHAVIOR & CARE: Nerites do not produce viable young in fresh water. They lay small, sesame-seed-sized eggs, generally on hardscape, that do not usually hatch. Young hatch into larvae, which will not develop in fresh water. They are completely peaceful, so they make beautiful and colorful additions to any community setup.

REDSPOT NERITE *Neritina semicona*
(Tracked Nerite)
NATIVE RANGE: Indonesia
MAXIMUM SIZE: 1.5 in. (4 cm)
MINIMUM AQUARIUM SIZE: 5 gal. (19 L)

BUMBLEBEE HORNED NERITE *Clithon corona, C. diadema*
(Mini Snail, Horned Nerite)
NATIVE RANGE: Philippines
MAXIMUM SIZE: 1.5 in. (4 cm)
MINIMUM AQUARIUM SIZE: 5 gal. (19 L)

ZEBRA NERITE *Neritina natalensis, N. turrita*
Tiger Nerite
NATIVE RANGE: Southeast Asia
MAXIMUM SIZE: 1.5 in. (4 cm)
MINIMUM AQUARIUM SIZE: 5 gal. (19 L)

BASEBALL HELMET NERITE *Neritina puligera*
Baseball Cap Nerite
NATIVE RANGE: Philippines
MAXIMUM SIZE: 1.5 in. (4 cm)
MINIMUM AQUARIUM SIZE: 5 gal. (19 L)

AFRICAN DWARF FROG *Hymenochirus boettgeri*
(Congo Dwarf Clawed Frog, ADF)

OVERVIEW: A petite, fully aquatic frog, this is a curiosity and an excellent choice for a small tank. Because they are surface breathers, they do best in a tank that is not very deep.

NATIVE RANGE: Cameroon, Gabon, Nigeria, Congo

MAXIMUM SIZE: 2.4 in. (6 cm)

MINIMUM AQUARIUM SIZE: 5 gal. (19 L)

WATER PARAMETERS: pH 7–8, 72–84°F (22–29°C)

FEEDING: Carnivore. They will thrive if offered a variety of frozen foods (bloodworms) and live foods (white worms) or small pelleted foods for carnivores. They are clumsy feeders who rely on their poor eyesight, so they often need to be target-fed using tongs or a baster.

BEHAVIOR & CARE: ADFs are clownish creatures, actively moving around the tank. They appreciate plants near the water's surface, like *Anubias*, which they will rest on between breaths. They are compatible with any community fishes that cannot fit in their mouths. They are commonly confused with the African Clawed Frog, but can be easily distinguished by examining their feet. The ADF has four webbed feet, while the Clawed Frog has webbed rear feet and individual clawed toes on the front. Because of their petite size and slender appendages, care should be taken not to combine ADFs with fishes that would attack their legs. These frogs can be bred. The male produces a song and has a small white or red spot behind the armpit; the female is noticeably rounder and plumper and has a small tail bud.

SPECIES INDEX

SPECIES INDEX

RECOMMENDED REFERENCES

Amano, T. 1994. *Nature Aquarium World*, Book 2. TFH Publications, Neptune City, NJ.

Amano, T. 1994. *Nature Aquarium World*, Book 3. TFH Publications, Neptune City, NJ.

Barber, T. and R. Wilson. 2005. *The Simple Guide to Planted Aquariums.* TFH Publications, Neptune City, NJ.

Evers, H.-G. and I. Seidel. 2005. *Catfish Atlas, Vol 1*. Baensch, Melle, Germany.

Fohrman, K., R. Toning, and J. Kienjet. 2010. *Back to Nature: Guide to Nano Aquaria*. Fohrman Aquaristik, Jonsered, Sweden.

Fuller, I.A.M. and H.-G. Evers. 2005. *Identifying Corydoradinae Catfishes*. IFE, Kidderminster, UK.

Hiscock, P. 2003. *Encyclopedia of Aquarium Plants*. Barron's Educational Series, Inc., Hauppauge, NY.

Kasselmann, Christel. 2003. *Aquarium Plants*. Krieger Publishing Company, Malabar, FL.

Rataj, K. and Horeman, T. 1977. *Aquarium Plants: Their Identification, Cultivation, and Ecology*. TFH Publications, Neptune City, NJ.

Scheurmann, I. 1987. *Water Plants in the Aquarium: A Complete Owner's Manual.* Barron's Educational Series, Inc., Hauppauge, NY.

Seidel, I. and H.-G. Evers. 2005. *Wels Atlas, Vol. 2*. Baensch, Melle, Germany.

Sweeney, M., M. Bailey, and A. Norman. 2009. *A PocketExpert Guide to Tropical Fishes.* Microcosm/TFH Publications, Neptune City, NJ.

Sweeney, M. 2008. *Adventurous Aquarist Guide: 101 Best Aquarium Plants.* Microcosm/TFH Publications, Neptune City, NJ.

Walstad, D.L. 1999. *Ecology of the Planted Aquarium.* Echinodorus Publishing, Chapel Hill, NC.

Wood, Kathleen. 2007. *Adventurous Aquarist Guide: 101 Best Tropical Fishes*. Microcosm/TFH Publications, Neptune City, NJ.

RESOURCES ONLINE

Aquatic Gardening Association www.aquatic-gardeners.org

Fish Base www.fishbase.org

Monster Fishkeepers www.monsterfishkeepers.com

Planet Catfish www.planetcatfish.com

Seriously Fish www.seriouslyfish.com

Biotope—in nature, a habitat with a distinctive assemblage of plants, animals, and environmental conditions; in aquarium-keeping, a system designed to replicate a biotope in the wild—e.g., a pool in a stream in Amazonia with plants and fishes often found together in that ecosystem.

Congener—a member of the same genus.

Consexual—a member of the same sex.

Conspecific—a member of the same species.

Cyclops—a tiny aquatic crustacean in the genus *Cyclops* that provides a color-enhancing, nutrient-rich food for nano- and juvenile fishes.

Daphnia—small planktonic crustaceans found in acidic swamps, lakes, ponds, and other bodies of fresh water. An excellent, high-protein food for nano- and juvenile fishes.

Dither fish—an active, bold fish that will swim in the water column and cause more timid species to become bolder.

Gut-packing—providing a live prey item (e.g., ghost shrimp, brine shrimp, mollies) with a nutritious food an hour or two before feeding them to your marine fishes.

Grindal worms—a classic live, cultured food for aquarium organisms. Also known as white worms, *Enchytraeus buchholzi*.

Heterospecific—a member of a different species.

Nano-aquarium—in freshwater aquaristics, often defined as a tank that holds 20 gallons (76 L) or less.

Pico aquarium—often defined as a tank with a volume of 5 gallons (19 L) or less.

School—a group of fishes, usually of equal size, that move and act as a single unit and are equal in social status.

Sexual dichromatism—color difference between the sexes.

Shoal—a group of fishes in which social attraction occurs, but individuals are not equal in social status and their movements are not as coordinated as a those of a school.

Species tank—an aquarium devoted to a single species of fish or invertebrate, often used for the purpose of breeding.

Zooplankton—free-floating, typically minute animals (e.g., protozoa, copepods, crustacean larvae, fish larvae).

PHOTOGRAPHY

RACHEL O'LEARY: 37, 58, 60, 61, 64, 65, 66, 67, 68, 82, 85 (bottom), 86, 89, 97, 130, 162, 163, 164, 166, 167, 168, 169, 170, 171, 172, 173, 175, 176, 177, 178, 180, 181, 182 (top), 183

AARON NORMAN: 43, 53, 54, 55, 56, 62, 63, 69, 71, 73, 74, 75, 80, 81, 84, 87, 92, 93, 96, 104, 109, 110, 122, 126, 127, 128, 129, 131, 134, 135

PAUL V. LOISELLE, PH.D.: 72, 77, 78, 79, 85 (top), 88, 94, 95, 99, 101, 102, 105, 108, 112, 115, 116, 124, 125

HANS-GEORG EVERS: 52, 57, 59, 70, 91, 100, 106, 111, 117, 118, 119, 123, 132, 137, 160, 174

GARY LANGE: 7, 41, 42, 83, 98, 103, 113, 114, 121, 136

BEN TAN, AQUASPOT WORLD: 140, 143, 144 (bottom), 149, 150, 158

SUMER TIWARI: 12, 19, 21, 31, 33, 38, 44, 50

MARK DENARO: 47, 51, 76, 90, 107, 120, 133, 147, 151, 154, 192 (left)

MP & C PIEDNOIR: 15, 17, 141, 144 (top), 145, 148, 156

CHRISTIAN PIEDNOIR: 22, 24, 25, 26, 27

FLORIDA AQUATIC NURSERY: 152, 155, 157

GEORGE FARMER: 153, 159

KRIS WEINHOLD: 28, 146

LEANDRO ARTIOLI: 138

ROLAND BLANKENHAUS: 165

MIKAEL HAKÅNSON: 179

OLIVER LUCANUS: 46

FELICIA MCCAULLEY: 192 (right)

MATT PEDERSEN: 48

KHOR HARN SHENG: 53 | **FRANK STROZYK:** 49

STEVE WALDRON: 35

MAIKE WILSTERMANN-HILDEBRAND: 182 (bottom)

JEFF UCCIARDO: 28

MATTHEW L. WITTENRICH, PH.D.: 142

Mark Denaro has been keeping freshwater aquariums for more than four decades, and has bred and propagated over 300 species of freshwater fishes and aquatic plants. He has owned an aquarium shop, a saltwater wholesale operation, and several aquarium and terrarium installation and maintenance companies, as well as Anubias Design, an online retailer of fishes, invertebrates, and plants. He writes for *Tropical Fish Hobbyist* and other magazines. Mark is a past president of the International Betta Congress and is the inaugural president of the American Labyrinth Fish Association. He lives with his family in Bensalem, Pennsylvania.

Rachel O'Leary currently keeps more than 100 freshwater aquariums for her business, Invertebrates by Msjinkzd, catering to interests that run from the smallest invertebrates to primitive monster fishes like bichirs and gars. She uses a growing network of contacts around the globe to source many uncommon micro-fishes and dwarf freshwater invertebrates, including shrimp, snails, crayfishes, and aquatic crabs, for the American market. A firm believer in the importance of shared knowledge, Rachel is also an unforgettable and knowledgeable presence at national and international aquarium conferences and society events. She lives with her husband and two children in Mount Wolf, Pennsylvania.